iCONLOGiC™

Version: 030120
Page Count:140
ISBNs:
    9781944607579 (Perfect-Bound Print Book)
    9781944607586 (PDF)
    9781944607593 (Kindle eBook)

Notice: Although IconLogic makes every effort to ensure the accuracy and quality of these materials, all material is provided without any warranty.

Copyright: 2020 by IconLogic, Inc. This document, or any part thereof, may not be reproduced or transmitted in any form or by any means, electronic or mechanical, including photocopying, recording, storage in an information retrieval system, or otherwise, without the prior written permission of IconLogic.

Trademarks: IconLogic, Inc., and the IconLogic logo are registered trademarks of IconLogic. All companies and product names are trademarks or registered trademarks of their respective companies. They are used in this book in an editorial fashion only. No use of any trade name is intended to convey endorsement or other affiliation with IconLogic books.

iSpring Suite 9: The Essentials

"Skills and Drills" Learning

Kevin Siegel

iCONLOGiC

"Skills and Drills" Learning

Contents

NOTES

© 2020, IconLogic. All Rights Reserved.

Module 4: Interactivity and Screen Recordings

Module 5: Quizzing

Module 6: Publishing

NOTES

Notes

© 2020, IconLogic. All Rights Reserved.

ICONLOGIC

"Skills and Drills" Learning

About This Book

During This Module You Will Learn About:

The Author

Kevin Siegel is a Certified Master Trainer (CMT), Certified Technical Trainer (CTT+), and Certified Online Training Professional (COTP). Following a successful tour of duty with the U.S. Coast Guard (where Kevin was twice decorated with the Coast Guard's Achievement Medal), he has spent decades as a technical communicator, classroom and online trainer, eLearning developer, publisher, and public speaker. Kevin, who founded IconLogic, Inc., in the early 1990s, has written hundreds of training books for adult learners. Some of his best-selling books include "Adobe Captivate: The Essentials," "Articulate Storyline: The Essentials," and "TechSmith Camtasia: The Essentials." Kevin has also been recognized by Adobe as one of the top trainers worldwide.

IconLogic

Founded in 1992, IconLogic is a training, development, and publishing company offering services to clients across the globe.

As a **training** company, IconLogic has directly trained tens of thousands of professionals both on-site and online on dozens of applications. Our training clients include some of the largest companies in the world including: Adobe Systems, Inc., Urogen, Agilent, Sanofi Pasteur, Kelsey Seybold, FAA, Office Pro, Adventist Health Systems, AGA, AAA, Wells Fargo, VA.gov, American Express, Lockheed Martin, General Mills, Grange Insurance, Electric Boat, Michigan.gov, Freddie Mac, Fannie Mae, ADP, ADT, Federal Reserve Bank of Richmond, Walmart, Kroger, Duke Energy, USCG, USMC, Canadian Blood, PSA, Department of Homeland Security, and the Department of Defense.

As a **development** company, IconLogic has produced eLearning and technical documentation for Duke Energy, World Bank, Heineken, EverFi, Bank of America, Fresenius Kabi, Wells Fargo, Federal Express, Fannie Mae, American Express, Microsoft, Department of For-Hire Vehicles, DC Child and Family Services, DCORM, Canadian Blood, Cancer.org, MLB, Archrock, NEEF, CHUBB, Canadian Natural Resources, and Hagerty Insurance.

As a **publishing** company, IconLogic has published hundreds of critically acclaimed books and created technical documents for both print and digital publication. Some of our most popular titles over the years include books on HTML, Dreamweaver, QuarkXPress, PageMaker, InDesign, Word, Excel, Access, Publisher, RoboHelp, RoboDemo, iSpring, Presenter, Storyline, Captivate, and PowerPoint for eLearning.

You can learn more about IconLogic's varied services at www.iconlogic.com.

© 2020, IconLogic, Inc. All Rights Reserved.

Book Conventions

Learners learn best by doing, not just by watching or listening. With that concept in mind, instructors and authors with years of experience training adult learners have created IconLogic books. Each of our books contain a minimal amount of text and are loaded with hands-on activities, screen captures, and challenge exercises to reinforce newly acquired skills.

This book is divided into modules. Because each module builds on lessons learned in a previous module, it is recommended that you complete each module in succession.

Lesson Key

Instructions for you to follow look like this (the boxes are also used in bulleted lists):

❏ click this or do that

If you are expected to type anything or if something is important, it is set in bold type like this:

❏ type **9** into the **text field**

If you are expected to press a key on your keyboard, the instruction looks like this:

❏ press [**shift**]

Confidence Checks

As you move through the lessons in this book, you will come across the figure at the right. The figure indicates a **Confidence Check**. Throughout each module you will be guided through hands-on, step-by-step exercises. But at some point you'll have to fend for yourself. That is where Confidence Checks come in. Please be sure to complete each of the challenges because some exercises build on completed Confidence Checks.

NOTES

© 2020, IconLogic, Inc. All Rights Reserved.

System Requirements

This book teaches you how to use many, but not all, of the features of iSpring Suite 9. The iSpring Suite software does not come with this book. The software can be purchased and downloaded directly from iSpring (**www.ispringsolutions.com/ispring-suite**).

Although you need to have both **Microsoft PowerPoint** and **iSpring Suite** installed on your computer prior to starting the hands-on activities presented in this book, you **do not** need to purchase iSpring Suite to learn iSpring Suite. A free trial version of the software can be downloaded via iSpring's website. The iSpring Suite 9 trial has a few limitations, but it will work for a few weeks from the day you first start the program. Keep in mind that eLearning lessons that you create using the trial version of iSpring Suite will no longer open once the trial period expires. (Any projects you create with the trial will be available to edit and publish once you license the software.)

Here are the system requirements for installing and using iSpring Suite 9.

Hardware	
Computer and processor	Dual-Core processor (Quad-Core or higher is recommended, 2.0 GHz or faster)
Memory	4 GB (Recommended: 8 GB or more)
Free disk space	2 GB for installation and 20 GB for operation
Display	1366x768 or higher resolution
Video card	NVIDIA® GeForce® 8 series, Intel® HD Graphics 2000, or AMD Radeon™ R600 or higher with 512 MB memory for regular video and 1 GB for HD video, Direct3D 10.1/Direct 2D compatible graphics adapter is required for the correct work of iSpring Cam Pro.
Audio	Sound card and microphone (for narration recording)
Video	Built-in or external webcam (for video recording)
Software	
Operating System	Microsoft® Windows® 7/8/10 (32- and 64-bit)
Microsoft PowerPoint	Microsoft® PowerPoint® 2007/2010/2013/2016/2019 (32- and 64-bit)
Microsoft Word	Microsoft® Word® 2007/2010/2013/2016/2019 (32- and 64-bit)
Internet Explorer	Internet Explorer 9.0 or higher

© 2020, IconLogic, Inc. All Rights Reserved.

Data Files (iSpring Suite Project Assets)

You're probably chomping at the bit, ready to dive into iSpring Suite, and begin creating eLearning lessons. Not so fast. Do you have sample projects to work with? What about graphics and videos? How about voiceover audio? No? No worries. I've got everything you need—I call them data files—and they can be downloaded from the IconLogic website for free.

Download the iSpring Suite 9 Data Files

1. Download the student data files necessary to use with this book.

   ❏ start a web browser and go to the following web address:
   http://www.iconlogic.com/pc

   ❏ under the **iSpring Data Files** section, click the **iSpring Suite 9: The Essentials** link

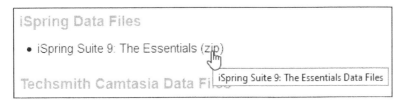

The download is a zipped file containing several folders and files. On most web browsers, a dialog box opens asking if you want to Save or Open the file. The image below shows the dialog box you will see if you use Firefox. I've elected to **Save File**.

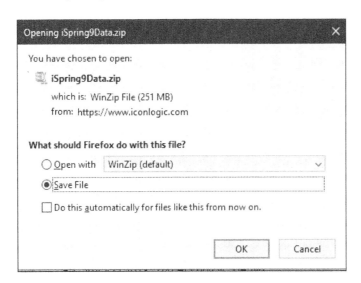

NOTES

© 2020, IconLogic, Inc. All Rights Reserved.

2. Unzip the **iSpring9Data** files.

   ☐ locate the **iSpring9Data.zip** file you just downloaded to your computer

   ☐ unzip the file

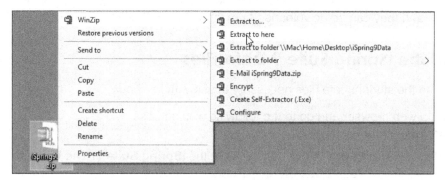

Note: You can keep the iSpring9Data folder anywhere on your computer, but for ease of access, I suggest working from your desktop so that it's easier to locate the project files as they are referenced during the guided activities in this book.

How Software Updates Affect This Book

This book was written to teach you how to use iSpring Suite **version 9** (you can check your version via the iSpring Suite tab on the Ribbon, **Help > About**). At the time that this book was written, iSpring Suite **9.7.7 Build 21094** was the latest and greatest version of the software available from iSpring.

With each major release of iSpring Suite, my intention is to write a new book to support that version and to make it available as soon as possible. Both Microsoft and iSpring frequently update their software to fix bugs and add functionality. Updated iSpring Suite versions could be called iSpring Suite **9.7.8** or **9.7.9** and so on. Usually minor updates have little or no impact on the lessons presented in this book. However, iSpring could make significant changes to the way the suite looks or behaves, even with minor updates. (Such was the case when Adobe updated its Adobe Captivate software from version 5 to 5.5—about a dozen features were added, and a few panels/pods were renamed, throwing readers of those books into a tizzy.)

Because it is not possible for me to recall or update existing printed books, instructions you are asked to follow in this book may not exactly match the patched/updated version of the software that you are using. If something on your screen does not match what is in the book, please visit the book errata page on my website (http://www.iconlogic.com/skills-drills-workbooks/errata-pages.html). If an iSpring software update has altered something that impacts the lessons in this book, I will address the issues on that page as they are brought to my attention.

Contacting IconLogic

Web: www.iconlogic.com
Email: ksiegel@iconlogic.com
Phone: 410.956.4949, ext 711

                                                    © 2020, IconLogic, Inc. All Rights Reserved.

iCONLOGiC

"Skills and Drills" Learning

Rank Your Skills

Before starting this book, complete the skills assessment on the next page.

Skills Assessment

How This Assessment Works

Ten course objectives for *iSpring Suite 9: The Essentials* are listed below. **Before starting the book**, review each objective and rank your skills using the scale next to each objective. A rank of ① means **No Confidence** in the skill. A rank of ⑤ means **Total Confidence**. After you've completed this assessment, work through the entire book. **After finishing the book**, review each objective and rank your skills now that you've completed the book. Most people see dramatic improvements in the second assessment after completing the lessons in this book.

Before-Class Skills Assessment

1. I can sync animations with voiceover.	①	②	③	④	⑤
2. I can add video to a presentation.	①	②	③	④	⑤
3. I can add a Dialog Simulation to a presentation.	①	②	③	④	⑤
4. I can add Characters to a slide.	①	②	③	④	⑤
5. I can add an interaction.	①	②	③	④	⑤
6. I can add a quiz to a presentation.	①	②	③	④	⑤
7. I know how to publish as HTML5.	①	②	③	④	⑤
8. I know what SCORM stands for.	①	②	③	④	⑤
9. I can edit audio files.	①	②	③	④	⑤
10. I can create a screen recording.	①	②	③	④	⑤

After-Class Skills Assessment

1. I can sync animations with voiceover.	①	②	③	④	⑤
2. I can add video to a presentation.	①	②	③	④	⑤
3. I can add a Dialog Simulation to a presentation.	①	②	③	④	⑤
4. I can add Characters to a slide.	①	②	③	④	⑤
5. I can add an interaction.	①	②	③	④	⑤
6. I can add a quiz to a presentation.	①	②	③	④	⑤
7. I know how to publish as HTML5.	①	②	③	④	⑤
8. I know what SCORM stands for.	①	②	③	④	⑤
9. I can edit audio files.	①	②	③	④	⑤
10. I can create a screen recording.	①	②	③	④	⑤

iCONLOGiC

"Skills and Drills" Learning

Preface

This Section Covers:

iSpring Suite's Role in eLearning

It's likely that you've used Microsoft PowerPoint at least a little bit. As far as I'm concerned, PowerPoint is an awesome program, and you can easily create visually stunning presentations with the tool. Unfortunately, the vast majority of the presentations created with PowerPoint are not very good. I'm betting that you have seen your fair share of presentations containing too many slides packed with as much text and clipart as possible. There's often an obnoxious use of colors and fonts. The layouts are predictable and boring (most of the slides have a main headline, a subhead, a bulleted list, clipart images, and copious amounts of animation (the bullets fly here, there, everywhere). There's a name for those kinds of presentations: *Death by PowerPoint*.

When learners are threatened with *Death by PowerPoint*, most will simply click from one slide to the next, as quickly as possible to end the suffering sooner rather than later. There's typically little interaction in those deadly presentations beyond clicking forward and back buttons.

Given how PowerPoint gets most of the blame when someone presents a *Death by PowerPoint*, it's easy to be a PowerPoint hater. However, I am not a hater. I happen to think that in the hands of a creative person, PowerPoint can be used to develop great presentations. However, although I love PowerPoint, it cannot be used to create compelling, engaging eLearning (where asynchronous training content is available online, 24-hours per day, 7 days per week).

Why can't you create awesome eLearning with PowerPoint? First, PowerPoint does not feature the kind of interactive tools necessary to engage learners (sorry, but animations and/or forward and back buttons do not constitute a high level of interactivity). In most PowerPoint presentations, there's little to no opportunity to gauge learner comprehension of the content because most versions of PowerPoint do not include scoreable quizzes. (Recent versions of PowerPoint do allow you to add quizzes via Forms, but the feature is limited.)

When the time comes to deliver content created in PowerPoint to learners across the globe, there's no HTML5 output to fully support mobile learners. Learners either need to have PowerPoint installed on their computers or download the PowerPoint player from Microsoft. And although you can upload a PowerPoint presentation into a Learning Management System (LMS) as a course asset, there is no way to make the presentation SCORM or AICC-compliant so that learner progress can be tracked by the LMS or administrators.

So what do you do when the boss tells you to use PowerPoint to create the company's flagship eLearning course? You get yourself an eLearning development tool, and that's where the iSpring Suite comes in. The suite is a collection of awesome tools that work with PowerPoint to help you create killer eLearning courses.

After installing the iSpring Suite on your computer and then starting PowerPoint, you'll find that there's a new tab on the PowerPoint Ribbon: **iSpring Suite**. The image below shows the iSpring Suite tab, along with its specific set of eLearning tools.

At the **far left** of the **iSpring Suite 9** tab, you'll find recording tools for both audio and video. As you move right, you'll see tools for adding interactions, characters, and more. You'll be using most of the tools on the tab (along with the standard PowerPoint tools) as you move through the guided activities in this book.

© 2020, IconLogic, Inc. All Rights Reserved.

Designing Slides Within PowerPoint

As mentioned earlier, working with iSpring Suite means you also need to work within PowerPoint. It stands to reason that the better your PowerPoint presentation looks, the more likely it is that your learners will want to consume the content you publish.

I saw a guy the other day wearing a t-shirt that read, "Guns don't kill people, people kill people." Often the same holds true for PowerPoint presentations. "PowerPoint doesn't kill presentations; people kill presentations."

It's easy to point the finger at PowerPoint for making office meetings unsuccessful and presentations a snore, but the truth is that poor design is really to blame.

The good news is that you don't have to be a seasoned designer to produce beautiful and effective PowerPoint presentations. Here are a few tips to get you started:

- ❐ There are certainly occasions when a bullet really is the most successful way to convey an idea. However, just because PowerPoint defaults to using a bulleted format doesn't mean that you should go with the flow and present all your information with a bullet in front of it.

- ❐ Try splitting the bullets up into separate slides with a single image to illustrate each point, or forgo the text altogether and replace it with a chart, diagram, or other informative image.

- ❐ It is not necessary to have every bit of information you cover on the slide. Encourage your audience to listen and, if necessary, take notes based on what you say, not what is displayed on the slide.

- ❐ Nothing says "High School Presentation Circa 1997" quite like a dancing animated image clumsily plopped on a rainbow gradient background with a big, garish WordArt title (complete with myriad animation effects).

- ❐ Keep in mind that PowerPoint presentations are plentiful—particularly bad ones. Trust us, your learner will not be impressed with how many moving, colorful parts each slide contains.

- ❐ Consider using photographs on your slides instead of clipart. PowerPoint comes preloaded with photographs you can use. And there is an extensive set of backgrounds, images, and icons that come with iSpring Suite.

  If you find the selection isn't enough to suit your needs, try looking online for stock photos. There are many free sites, but keep in mind that to save time and frustration (and improve on the selection and quality), you might want to set aside a budget to pay for the photographs.

NOTES

Fonts and Learning

There is no denying that the most important thing about eLearning is solid content. But could you be inadvertently making your content harder to read and understand by using the wrong fonts? Is good font selection really important? Read on to discover the many surprising ways fonts can affect your content.

Some Fonts Read Better On-Screen

eCommerce Consultant Dr. Ralph F. Wilson did a study in 2001 to determine if serif fonts (fonts with little lines on the tops and bottoms of characters, such as Times New Roman) or sans serif fonts (those without lines, such as Arial) were more suited to being read on computer monitors. His study concluded that although Times New Roman is easily read in printed materials, the lower resolution of monitors (72 dpi vs 180 dpi or higher) makes it much more difficult to read in digital format. Arial 12 pt was pitted against Times New Roman 12 pt with respondents finding the sans serif Arial font more readable at a rate of 2-to-1.

Lorem ipsum frangali puttuto rigali fortuitous confulence magficati alorem. Lorem ipsum frangali puttuto rigali fortuitous confulence magficati alorem.	Lorem ipsum frangali puttuto rigali fortuitous confulence magficati alorem. Lorem ipsum frangali puttuto rigali fortuitous confulence magficati alorem.
Times New Roman 12 pt	Arial 12 pt
520	1123
32%	68%

Wilson also tested the readability of Arial vs. Verdana on computer screens and found that in font sizes greater than 10 pt, Arial was more readable, whereas Verdana was more readable in font sizes 10 pt and smaller.

So should you stop using Times New Roman in your eLearning lessons? Not completely. For instance, you can still use Times New Roman for text content that is not expected to be skimmed.

Some Fonts Increase Trust

A study by **Sharath Sasidharan** and **Ganga Dhanesh** for the Association of Information Systems found that typography can affect trust in eCommerce. The study found that to instill trust in online consumers, you should keep it simple: "To the extent possible, particularly for websites that need to engage in financial transactions or collect personal information from their users, the dominant typeface used to present text material should be a serif or sans serif font such as Times New Roman or Arial."

If you feel your eLearning content will be presented to a skeptical audience (or one you've never worked with before), dazzling them with fancy fonts may not be the way to go. I'm not saying that you shouldn't use fancy fonts from time to time to break up the monotony of a dry lesson, but consider using such nonstandard fonts sparingly. Use the fancy fonts for headings or as accents but not for the bulk of your text.

The Readability of Fonts Affects Participation

A study done at the **University of Michigan** in 2008 on typecase in instructions found that the ease with which a font in instructional material is read can have an impact on the perceived skill level needed to complete a task.

© 2020, IconLogic, Inc. All Rights Reserved.

The study found that if directions are presented in a font that is deemed more difficult to read, "the task will be viewed as being difficult, taking a long time to complete and perhaps, not even worth trying."

Based upon the aforementioned study by Wilson, it is probably not a good idea to present eLearning material, especially to beginners, in a Times New Roman font, as it may make the information seem too difficult to process or overwhelming.

Most Popular Fonts

I polled my "Skills & Drills" newsletter readers and asked which fonts they tended to use in eLearning. Here is a list of the most popular fonts:

- ❏ Verdana
- ❏ Helvetica
- ❏ Arial
- ❏ Calibri
- ❏ Times
- ❏ Palatino
- ❏ Times New Roman
- ❏ Century Schoolbook (for print)

© 2020, IconLogic, Inc. All Rights Reserved.

Fonts and Personas

If you are creating eLearning for business professionals, you might want to use a different font in your design than you would if you were creating eLearning for high school students. But what font would you use if you wanted to convey a feeling of happiness? Formality? Cuddliness?

In a study (funded by Microsoft) by **A. Dawn Shaikh**, **Barbara S. Chaparro**, and **Doug Fox**, the perceived personality traits of fonts were categorized. The table below shows the top three fonts for each personality objective.

	Top Three		
Stable	TNR	Arial	Cambria
Flexible	Kristen	Gigi	Rage Italic
Conformist	Courier New	TNR	Arial
Polite	Monotype Corsiva	TNR	Cambria
Mature	TNR	Courier New	Cambria
Formal	TNR	Monotype Corsiva	Georgia
Assertive	**Impact**	**Rockwell Xbold**	Georgia
Practical	Georgia	TNR	Cambria
Creative	Gigi	Kristen	Rage Italic
Happy	Kristen	Gigi	Comic Sans
Exciting	Gigi	Kristen	Rage Italic
Attractive	Monotype Corsiva	Rage Italic	Gigi
Elegant	Monotype Corsiva	Rage Italic	Gigi
Cuddly	Kristen	Gigi	Comic Sans
Feminine	Gigi	Monotype Corsiva	Kristen
Unstable	Gigi	Kristen	Rage Italic
Rigid	**Impact**	Courier New	Agency FB
Rebel	Gigi	Kristen	Rage Italic
Rude	**Impact**	**Rockwell Xbold**	Agency FB
Youthful	Kristen	Gigi	Comic Sans
Casual	Kristen	Comic Sans	Gigi
Passive	Kristen	Gigi	Comic Sans
Impractical	Gigi	Rage Italic	Kristen
Unimaginative	Courier New	Arial	Consolas
Sad	**Impact**	Courier New	Agency FB
Dull	Courier New	Consolas	Verdana
Unattractive	**Impact**	Courier New	**Rockwell Xbold**
Plain	Courier New	**Impact**	**Rockwell Xbold**
Coarse	**Impact**	**Rockwell Xbold**	Courier New
Masculine	**Impact**	**Rockwell Xbold**	Courier New

Source: http://usabilitynews.org/perception-of-fonts-perceived-personality-traits-and-uses/

© 2020, IconLogic, Inc. All Rights Reserved.

Planning eLearning Projects

By the time you finish the last lesson in this book, you should be able to use the Suite to create some compelling, technically sound eLearning lessons. However, just because you will soon be able to publish technically sound content does not necessarily mean you will go out and create *good* eLearning. If you want to create good, useful lessons, you have to plan ahead. Before creating an eLearning lesson using iSpring Suite, ask yourself the following questions:

❑ Who is my audience? Are you training children or business professionals? The images you use and the interactions you create will need to take your specific audience into consideration.

❑ How is my eLearning content relevant to my learner? Will my content motivate my learners? Is there an appropriate amount of context?

❑ Is my content expected to bring about change? If yes, what specific change(s)? How do I plan to track that change?

❑ Do I want my lessons to contain images and background music? If so, where will I get those assets? While iSpring Suite comes with a ton of free assets if you have a subscription, those assets may not be enough. In that case, you'll need a reliable source for gathering additional assets. For instance, I use pay services such as www.BigStock.com for many of the images I use in my eLearning lessons. I also rely heavily on eLearning resources, such as www.eLearningBrothers.com for assets appropriate for eLearning.

❑ Do you need to capture learner data such as quizzes? If so, you'll likely need an LMS. You'll learn more about LMSs beginning on page 116.

When planning projects, keep in mind that the most useful lessons contain the following basic elements:

❑ Title slide (telling the learner what they are going to learn)

❑ Lesson slides containing narration, music, and other sound effects

❑ Images and animations

❑ As much interactivity as possible (via interactions and buttons)

❑ A quiz (to gauge the effectiveness of the lesson)

❑ An ending slide (reviewing what the learner learned)

Above all, remember the mantra used in the best training courses world-wide: *tell them what you're going to teach them, teach them, and then tell them what you taught them.* If your eLearning content created with iSpring Suite takes this mantra into account, there's a very good chance you'll not just create eLearning content, you'll create successful eLearning content.

NOTES

eLearning Budgeting Considerations

Many new eLearning developers underestimate the time needed to produce eLearning content with PowerPoint and iSpring Suite. The following table should help.

Project Size	Number of Production Hours
Small Projects (1-20 slides)	1-4 hours
Medium Projects (21-40 slides)	5-7 hours
Large Projects (41-70 slides)	8-10 hours
Bloated Projects (more than 71- slides)	Consider splitting lessons this large into smaller presentations.

I bet you're wondering what "production" means, especially considering the fact that most of the projects you create will likely be in the medium or large categories (21-70 slides) and take you, on average, up to 10-hours to produce.

What Production Does Not Include

To begin, let's consider what "production" does **not** include. An effective 1-hour eLearning course will not play for 60 consecutive minutes. Given today's distractions, the perfect playtime for any one eLearning lesson is between 3 and 7 minutes (a 5-minute playtime is ideal). A 5-minute playtime means that a 60-minute eLearning course would consist of 12, 5-minute lessons.

Before you can even think about creating an eLearning course, you'll need a script and/or storyboard (see page 10). A general rule of thumb is that it takes up to 40 hours to write every 1 hour of eLearning. Depending on how fast you write, you could easily save some time here (if you're a fast writer). However, you could also double those hours if you're new to creating eLearning content (or perhaps you simply write slowly).

If you're going to include voiceover audio (see page 40), you'll first need to write a voiceover script. Many writers budget at least 50 percent of the time it takes to write a standard script to write a voiceover script. And some writers say that writing a voiceover script is just as difficult as, if not more difficult than, writing a step-by-step eLearning script. To be safe, you should budget the same number of hours to write a voiceover script as you budget for the eLearning script.

Production won't include creating a PowerPoint template, a completed shell project that you will use as the basis of all of your projects. It's not difficult to create a template, but it will take time. An ideal template contains placeholders, an introduction slide, transitional slides, a conclusion slide, and a quiz placeholder. I typically budget up to 10 hours to create a project template.

What Production Does Include

A single interactive PowerPoint/iSpring Suite eLearning lesson could take several hours to produce. What's part of the production process?

You'll spend a lot of time working with every PowerPoint slide. Adding the content and the images will take time. Beyond the slide content and images, you'll be adding interactive objects. You'll also likely be adding audio to the presentation (if you're lucky, the audio won't need any editing, but it's likely you'll need to spend time editing the audio).

To measure the success of your eLearning lesson, you'll need a quiz. It's going to take time to write the questions, the answers, and the distractors. If you've never written questions and answers for a quiz, it's not as easy as you think. And it's going to take time. You should budget 15-20 minutes per question (and keep in mind that the average eLearning lesson should contain no more than one question for each minute of eLearning playtime).

© 2020, IconLogic, Inc. All Rights Reserved.

During the production process, you'll be previewing your project... a lot. That takes time (you cannot do any work in iSpring as the preview is created).

When your work is done, you'll publish the project and possibly upload the published assets files to a web server or LMS. You will be testing the lessons for scoring or interactivity errors. After that, you'll need to fix problems you run across (and there will likely be plenty of problems that need to be fixed). After fixing those problems, you'll need to republish, repost, and retest.

Add it all up, and your budget looks something like this (keep in mind that the timing below does not include the time it will take to record and edit your own voiceover audio):

- ❑ 40-80 hours to write an eLearning script or create the storyboard to support 12, 5-minute lessons for a 1-hour course.

- ❑ 120 hours to edit, produce and test 12, 5-minute lessons for a 1-hour eLearning course.

- ❑ 40-80 hours to write a narration script to be used by your narrator.

NOTES

Scripts for Software Demonstrations

When developing eLearning for software demonstrations or simulations (using eLearning tools like Adobe Captivate), it's a great idea to begin with a script—a detailed list of step-by-step instructions. When I have created text-based eLearning scripts, or received them from clients, I've generally seen them in two flavors: paragraphs and tables.

Scripts in Paragraph Format: If you are creating a script for eLearning, your text should be formatted in a way that is easy to follow. You can format the script in paragraphs, but you will need to clearly label the parts. You may find that formatted paragraphs are all you need. However, I recommend a table or grid format for a script that will be developed into eLearning.

- ☐ **Step Number**

- ☐ **Screen:** Display the document

- ☐ **Action:** Move the cursor to the Format menu and click Format

- ☐ **Caption:** Click Format

- ☐ **Voiceover:** Now let's open the Format menu to get started with formatting the document.

Scripts in Table Format: Below is a picture of a sample script used to create an Adobe Captivate eLearning lesson. The script was created in Microsoft Word. You'll find the script among the assets within the iSpring9Data folder (the file is called **SampleScript**).

Sample Script for Recording Captivate eLearning

Movie Name: Print a NotePad File with Landscape Orientation

Step	Screen	Action to be Taken by Captivate Developer	Caption Text	Narrator Says
1)	A NotePad file should be open prior to recording. You can start NotePad by choose Start > Run and typing notepad. Any open NotePad document can be used for this simulation.	Pull a screen shot of the NotePad file do not click anything. This slide will contain some introductory narrative.	During this lesson you will learn how to print a NotePad document	During this lesson you will learn how to print a NotePad document in Landscape Orientation.
2)	A NotePad file is open. Nothing should be selected and no menus should be open.	Click the **File** menu	First, let's display the Print dialog box. Choose **File > Print**.	To begin, let's display the Print dialog box by choosing the Print command from the File menu.
3)	The File menu is open.	Click the **Print** command	Select the Print command	
4)	Print Dialog Box with NotePad in the background	Select the HP4000 printer icon	The Print Dialog Box appears. Before you can print, you will need to select the correct printer. Select the **HP4000** printer icon.	The Print Dialog Box appears. Before you can print, you will need to select the correct printer. Select the HP4000 printer.

IconLogic Sample eLearning Script

© 2020, IconLogic, Inc. All Rights Reserved.

Storyboarding for Soft Skills

When the training objective is a soft skill, such as how to interact with others in the workplace or how to comply with legally required behavior, there may be no step-by-step process to spell out. Instead, you have to describe and demonstrate the behavior in a way that engages the learner. This is where the screen writing part of writing training materials comes into play.

You can present soft skills, which is typically what iSpring Suite is used to create, through slides or videos. Either way, the material must be both clear and engaging.

Here is a typical plotline for soft skills training.

- ☐ Statement of a real-world problem, challenge, or requirement

- ☐ Illustration of what happens on failure

- ☐ Demonstration and description of how to succeed

- ☐ Confidence check or evaluation

A visual storyboard allows you to plan what is pictured or acted out as well as what is said for each slide or scene. Even if you are not an artist, you can sketch the basics of the characters, setting, and behavior for each scene. In fact, take a look at the image below. I think that you will agree that the image is not a work of art. Nevertheless, you can tell that it depicts two people meeting in the reception area of an office. Even if the images mean something entirely different to you, you will be writing the script for these images in the Confidence Check that follows.

Slide/ Scene No.	Picture	Voiceover	Action	Dialogue
1				
2	*Recept.*			
3	*Rece*			

© 2020, IconLogic, Inc. All Rights Reserved.

Storyboard Confidence Check

Here are the visual storyboards for a training unit on how to greet a visitor to your office. Write the script for these scenes. Include a voiceover for each scene, briefly describe the action, and create dialog for the two actors in each scene as well. Some screens will have voiceover only.

Objective:

At the end of this lesson, you will be able to list at least four key behaviors in welcoming a guest to your office. In addition, you will have developed a specific plan for how to do this in your own office setting.

Slide/ Scene No.	Picture	Voiceover	Action	Dialogue
1				
2				
3				
4				
5				
6				

© 2020, IconLogic, Inc. All Rights Reserved.

7				
8	**Test Yourself** List at least four things to do when welcoming a guest to your office. 1. _____ 2. _____ 3. _____ 4. _____			
9	**Plan Ahead** 1. Where is your coat closet or rack? _____ 2. Where in your office can you take a visitor to get coffee, soda, or water? _____			

10	**Conclusion**			

NOTES

NOTES

Suggested Answers

#				
1		Don't let social awkwardness keep you from making a good first impression on your client. When a client comes to your office, you'll want to make sure to put them at their ease. Knowing the social niceties and having a plan will help you welcome a guest to your office with confidence. That will put your mind at ease, too!	Ellen and Jeff look uncomfortable and unhappy.	None
2		When you enter the reception area to welcome your guest, make sure to smile.	Ellen enters the reception area and smiles Seeing her smile, Jeff also smiles.	Ellen: Hi! You must be Jeff.
3		Make sure to introduce yourself.	Ellen shakes hands with Jeff	Ellen: I'm Ellen Jones. Its nice to meet you. Jeff: Jeff Barnes. It's nice to meet you too.
4		A proper business handshake is firm and brief. The handshake is a very important part of a proper business greeting.	Focus on handshake	
5		If your guest has an overcoat, offer to take his coat or allow him to hang it on a rack or in a closet.	Ellen takes Jeff's coat and hangs it up in the coat closet.	Ellen: Here's our coat closet. May I take your overcoat? You can retrieve it here after our meeting. Jeff: Yes, thanks!
6		It is also customary to offer your guest coffee, water, or another beverage.	Ellen and Jeff enter the employee lounge, where Ellen points to the coffee and soda machines.	Ellen: Would you care for some coffee or a soda? Jeff: Oh, no thanks. I'm good.

© 2020, IconLogic, Inc. All Rights Reserved.

7		Once you arrive at your office, make sure to offer your guest a chair.	Ellen and Jeff arrive in Ellen's office. Ellen gestures toward the guest chair.	Ellen: Please have a seat right over here.
8	**Test Yourself** List at least four things to do when welcoming a guest to your office. 1. _____ 2. _____ 3. _____ 4. _____	Now that you have seen Ellen welcome Jeff to the office, what did you observe? List here four things you can do to welcome a guest or client into your office.		
9	**Plan Ahead** 1. Where is your coat closet or rack? _____ 2. Where in your office can you take a visitor to get coffee, soda, or water? _____	Use this opportunity to plan how you will welcome clients into your office. Do you have a coat rack or closet? Where can you take your visitor to get coffee, soda, tea, or water?		
10	**Conclusion**	By having a plan for welcoming clients to your office, you will be all set to start each new business relationship on a comfortable basis and create a positive experience for each new client.		

NOTES

© 2020, IconLogic, Inc. All Rights Reserved.

The Value of Audio

You'll learn how to record, import, and edit audio files beginning on page 43. Research has shown that voiceover audio, even if it isn't highly produced, enhances the learning experience when compared to eLearning lessons with no audio. If your budget allows, the ideal way to approach audio is to write a voiceover script and then send the script to a voiceover professional. The cost to work with a professional can vary from state to state and region to region. I've seen audio cost as little as a few pennies per word, to several dollars per word. Still other voiceover professionals don't charge by the word at all, they charge by the page.

If you prefer to record the audio yourself, you do not need to have any prior experience recording audio. Nor do you need to have a deep, radio-personality voice. In fact, regular everyday people record perfectly wonderful audio every day. And you'll soon discover that recording audio (or importing audio files) from within iSpring Suite is very easy. All you really need to record audio is a microphone either hooked up to your computer or built-in. (While some built-in microphones record audio very well, you'll almost always get better results if you use an external microphone or headset.)

Should Voiceover Audio Match the Screen Text?

I spoke to an eLearning student who relayed a frustrating experience she had with an eLearning lesson. The learner needed information about Cascading Style Sheets. She accessed a training site and played an eLearning demo that explained how to redefine an HTML tag. During the video, the learner found herself both listening to the voiceover audio and reading the text on the screen. She quickly realized that the slide text was identical to the voiceover audio. At about the same time, because she had been trying to figure out whether the voiceover really was the same as the slide text, the learner realized that she had not absorbed some of the content. She also noticed that she could read the text on the screen faster than the narrator, so she turned off the audio and just read the rest of the slide text.

The learner had just experienced first-hand what I have heard from fellow eLearning developers over the years: screen text that is identical to the voiceover narration can be a distraction rather than an added value to the learning process. The best scenario is to have graphics, animation, or video accompanied by voiceover—with little or no text on the screen at all. Because learners are trying to pay attention to the visuals, the need to move their eyes to focus on the accompanying screen text is a distraction. Having a voiceover explain the visuals enables the learner to absorb the audio and visual information at the same time.

In the end, the learner told us that the decision to turn off the audio was a mistake. She felt that she would have had a better learning experience if she had listened to the audio while focusing on the videos and ignoring the printed captions at the bottom of the screen.

Does that mean your PowerPoint slides should never include text or bulleted lists? Of course not. Sometimes screen text is required simply because there is no voiceover or the learner may not have access to the voiceover.

Other times when text should appear on screen are:

- ❏ When there is no visual graphic and the caption text is the only information being presented

- ❏ When the text is closely integrated with the graphics—as labels rather than separate descriptions

- ❏ When the information being covered is complex and benefits from both audio and visual presentation, as with math equations or chemical formulas

- ❏ When the information may be needed over time, as in instructions for a learning exercise where the learner may need to repeatedly refer to the instructions

© 2020, IconLogic, Inc. All Rights Reserved.

Module 1: Getting Started

In This Module You Will Learn About:

- iSpring Suite Interface, page 18
- Characters, page 26
- Backgrounds and Templates, page 33

And You Will Learn To:

- Explore an Existing PowerPoint Presentation, page 19
- Publish Content to the iSpring Cloud, page 23
- Insert and Resize a Character, page 26
- Insert a Background, page 33
- Insert Template Slides, page 36

iSpring Suite Interface

As mentioned in the Preface (page 2), iSpring Suite is an eLearning development companion for Microsoft PowerPoint. You access the tools that comprise the iSpring Suite two ways: via the **iSpring Suite tab** on the PowerPoint Ribbon or start iSpring Suite's Quick Start via the Windows Start menu (shown below).

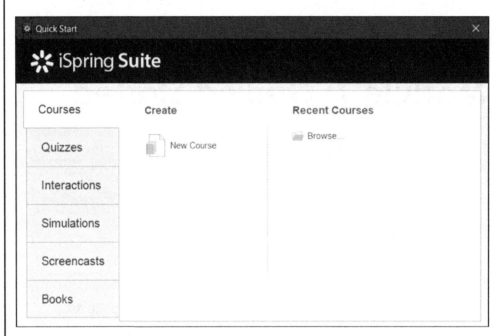

Courses: Creates a blank PowerPoint presentation. You'll create a course from scratch beginning on page 33.

Quizzes: Adds an interactive quiz to a PowerPoint presentation that can be set up to report scores to a Learning Management Systems (LMS). You'll learn about quizzes beginning on page 98.

Interactions: Adds interactive objects to PowerPoint slides. You'll learn about interactions beginning on beginning page 76.

Simulations: Creates branching scenarios/dialog simulations. You'll learn about this feature beginning on page 82.

Screencasts: Creates software video demonstrations including some nifty annotations. You'll learn about this feature beginning on page 91.

Books: Creates a slick-looking book from a PowerPoint presentation, Word document, or PDF. You'll publish a book during a Confidence Check on page 122.

During the first few guided activities in this book, you'll open an existing presentation created collaboratively with PowerPoint and iSpring Suite. You'll then have an opportunity to get comfortable with some of the tools unique to the iSpring Suite tab on the PowerPoint Ribbon.

> **Note:** Before moving forward, ensure that you have downloaded and installed the **iSpring9Data** assets as directed in the **About This Book** section of this book (page viii). You'll also need to ensure that you have Microsoft PowerPoint 2007 or higher on your computer (PowerPoint 365 is shown in the images throughout this book) and that you have installed iSpring Suite 9 or higher. (Review the "System Requirements" section that begins on page viii.)

© 2020, IconLogic, Inc. All Rights Reserved.

Guided Activity 1: Explore an Existing PowerPoint Presentation

1. Using Microsoft PowerPoint, open the **AquoSafetyDemo.pptx** presentation from the **iSpring9Data** folder.

   The **AquoSafetyDemo** presentation was created using standard features found in PowerPoint combined with iSpring Suite's tools. At first glance, the presentation looks like any other PowerPoint presentation. As mentioned in the Preface of this book, iSpring Suite's relationship within PowerPoint seems subtle, as the only apparent change to the PowerPoint interface is the addition of the iSpring Suite tab on the Ribbon (shown highlighted below).

2. Use the iSpring Suite tab on the Ribbon to preview the eLearning lesson.

   ☐ on the **PowerPoint Ribbon**, select the **iSpring Suite 9** tab

   ☐ on the **iSpring Suite** tab, click the **Preview** drop-down menu and choose **Preview Entire Presentation**

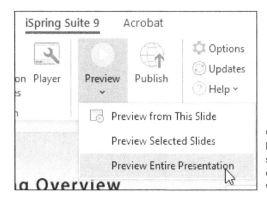

Generally speaking, when you click the bottom half of a tool within PowerPoint, you'll see a menu of options. If you click the top part of the tool, you'll select the most common item within the menu.

© 2020, IconLogic, Inc. All Rights Reserved.

A preview of the presentation appears that looks and behaves much as it would if you published the lesson.

The presentation contains images, videos, audio, and a quiz. You will learn how to work with these kinds of features as you work through the lessons in this book.

Note: If there are iSpring components in a PowerPoint presentation (such as an iSpring quiz or an interaction), they will not appear in the presentation if iSpring Suite is not installed on the computer. When it comes to previewing, iSpring components will not preview in a standard PowerPoint Slide Show. You can only preview iSpring components when the presentation is previewed using iSpring (**iSpring Suite 9** tab on the Ribbon **> Preview.**)

3. Spend a few moments going through the presentation.

4. When finished, close the preview window.

© 2020, IconLogic, Inc. All Rights Reserved.

5. Explore the iSpring Suite tool groups.

☐ at the far left of the **iSpring Suite** tab, observe the **Narration** group of tools

You'll use the tools in the **Narration** group to record, import, edit, and sync audio. You'll work with audio beginning on page 40.

☐ just to the right of the **Narration** group, observe the **Insert** group

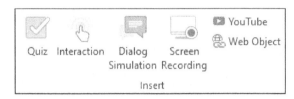

The **Insert** group gives you access to quizzes, interactions, screen recordings, and more. When it comes to adding some awesome interactive components to your project, this is the place to look.

☐ still working on the **iSpring Suite** tab, notice the **Content Library** group

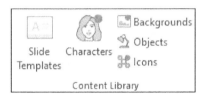

As you build your projects, you'll come to appreciate the Content Library where you find a collection of templates, icons, and characters that you can use on your slide. Access to these assets is included with the iSpring Suite subscription (www.ispringsolutions.com/ispring-suite).

☐ on the iSpring Suite tab, notice the **Presentation** group

The Presentation group lets you control how each of the slides in the presentation behaves. Do you want them to be clickable? Do you want them to move forward by themselves? How about building a branching scenario? You'll control all of the options via Slide Properties. If there are resources you'd like to add to your presentation or you'd like to include your corporate logo, you'll find the options available in the Presentation Resources. And the Player allows you to include an Outline, Notes, and more.

☐ on the iSpring Suite tab, notice the **Publish** group

There are two options in the Publish group: Preview and Publish. You've already used the Preview icon to see how your eLearning content will look if you publish it. The Publish feature is something you'll use if your project is finished and you're ready to make it available for your learners.

☐ on the iSpring Suite tab, notice the **About** group

The **Options** icon allows you to set up your microphone and webcam. **Updates** helps to ensure that you're running the latest and greatest version of iSpring Suite. **Help** gives you access to, among other things, a wonderful Community of like-minded eLearning developers and professionals who answer iSpring Suite questions. The Help menu's **About** option lets you know which version of iSpring Suite you're currently using and provides information about the license.

© 2020, IconLogic, Inc. All Rights Reserved.

Guided Activity 2: Publish Content to the iSpring Cloud

1. Ensure that the **AquoSafetyDemo.pptx** presentation is still open.

2. Open the Publish dialog box.

   ❑ from the **Publish** group on the iSpring Suite tab, click **Publish**

   The **Publish** dialog box opens. This is the dialog box you will use once you have finished creating your eLearning lesson using iSpring Suite. To create eLearning content, you need both Microsoft PowerPoint and iSpring Suite. Before learners can use your content, you need to publish the presentation and then upload it to a web server, to **iSpring Cloud**, or to a LMS such as **iSpring Learn**.

3. Review the options when publishing locally.

   ❑ from the categories at the left of the Publish dialog box, click **My Computer**

   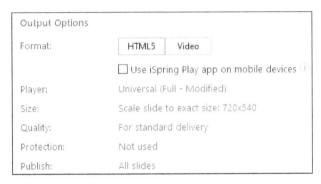

   You can Output your content as **HTML5** or as a **Video**. If you publish your content as HTML5 and upload the output files to a server, it remains interactive when accessed by learners. If you publish as a video, interactivity that you've added to the presentation (such as a quiz) won't work.

4. Publish to **iSpring Cloud**.

   ❑ from the categories at the left of the Publish dialog box, click **iSpring Cloud**

   iSpring Cloud provides a space for you to publish your course so it can be accessed by learners. It's free to set up a trial account and is subscription based.

   ❑ click the **right arrow** until you arrive at the **Start Now** screen (if this isn't the first time you've visited this screen, you'll likely end up on the login screen right away)

   ❑ click the **Start Now** button

© 2020, IconLogic, Inc. All Rights Reserved.

❑ fill in the account fields as necessary and create your account (or sign in if you already have an account)

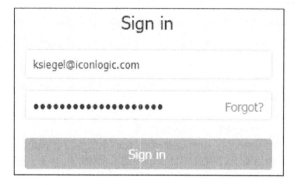

After signing in, you're ready to publish the project.

❑ accept all of the default settings and click the **Publish** button

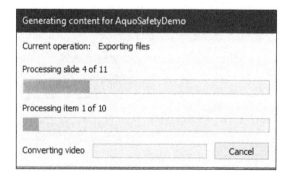

© 2020, IconLogic, Inc. All Rights Reserved.

The project is published and automatically uploaded to **iSpring Cloud**.

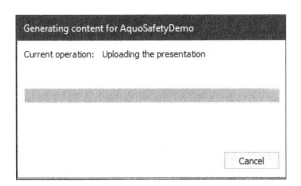

And just like that, you're a published eLearning author. Congratulations!

❏ click the **View Course** button

The course opens in your default web browser.

5. Close the browser window.

6. Return to PowerPoint and close the Publishing Complete screen.

7. Close the AquoSafetyDemo presentation. (There is no need to save the presentation if prompted.)

© 2020, IconLogic, Inc. All Rights Reserved.

Characters

Finding quality, royalty-free photographs is always a challenge, especially if you're looking for people that you can use throughout your iSpring Suite projects as guides. Fortunately, iSpring Suite comes with a wonderful assortment of Characters that are free to use in your iSpring projects.

> **Note:** iSpring trial has limited Content Library. The full suite license is needed to access all the Content Library assets.

Guided Activity 3: Insert and Resize a Character

1. Using Microsoft PowerPoint, open **CharacterMe** from the iSpring9Data folder.

2. Insert a Character onto slide 2.

   ☐ go to slide **2**

   ☐ on the Ribbon, click the **iSpring Suite 9** tab

   ☐ from the **Content Library** group, click **Characters**

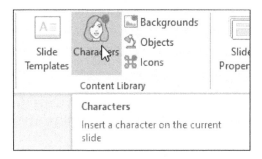

The Characters dialog box opens.

   ☐ in the Search box, type **Samantha** and press [**enter**]

The catalog of images is filtered to show only those images named by iSpring as Samantha.

   ☐ select the **second** version of Samantha

Several poses appear.

© 2020, IconLogic, Inc. All Rights Reserved.

❏ select any pose that you think looks welcoming

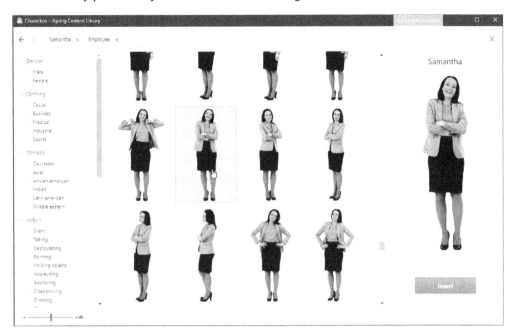

❏ click the **Insert** button

The selected Character appears in the middle of the slide.

3. Resize an image.

❏ on slide **2**, **right-click** Samantha and choose **Size and Position**

The **Format Picture** panel appears at the right of the PowerPoint window.

❏ change the **Scale height** to **30** and then press [**enter**]

Notice that because **Lock aspect ratio** is selected by default, the **Scale width** of the image automatically changes to **30**.

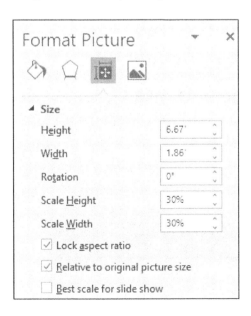

© 2020, IconLogic, Inc. All Rights Reserved.

NOTES

4. Reposition the image.

   ☐ drag Samantha to the left side of the slide until your slide is similar to the image below

Characters Confidence Check

1. Go to slide 3 and add another version of the Samantha character.

2. Resize and position the character at the left of the slide, similar to the positioning shown below.

3. Go to slide 6 and add a picture of Samantha facing left.

© 2020, IconLogic, Inc. All Rights Reserved.

4. Position the new character between the word **me** and the word **myself**.

5. Still working on slide 6, copy and paste the left-facing character to get a second copy.

6. Position the copied character directly on top of the original.

7. On the **Picture Format** tab of the PowerPoint Ribbon, click the **Rotate** drop-down menu and choose **Flip Horizontal**.

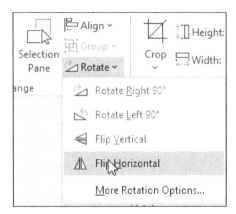

8. Position the two characters next to each other similar to the image below.

9. Select the **Home** tab on the Ribbon and, from the Editing group, click the Select drop-down menu and choose **Selection Pane**.

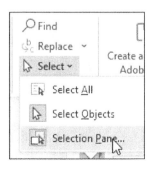

10. Select the first image and, on the Selection Pane, change the name of the image to **imageLeft**.

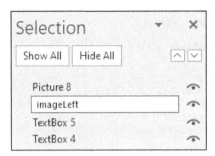

11. Change the name of the second image to **imageRight**.

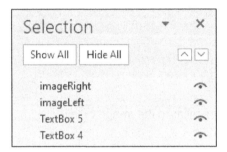

12. Change the name of the text box containing the word Me to **Me**.

13. Change the name of the text box containing the word Myself to **Myself**.

You're about to add animations to slide objects. Naming the objects makes it easier when it comes to work with them moving forward.

14. On the **Selection** pane, select both **imageLeft** and **Me**. (You can select noncontiguous objects by pressing [**ctrl**] and clicking the objects on the **Selection** pane.)

15. Select the **Animations** tab on the Ribbon and select the **Fade** animation.

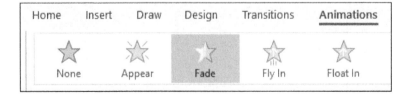

The selected objects now fade onto the slide. That'll be a nice effect but what will make it even better is to have both images fade out and then have the other two objects fade in. You'll take care of that next.

 © 2020, IconLogic, Inc. All Rights Reserved.

16. With both objects still selected, Select the **Animations** tab on the Ribbon and select **Add Animation**.

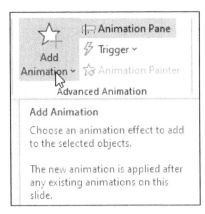

17. From the **Exit** animations, choose **Fade**.

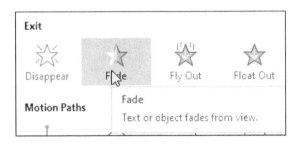

18. Using the **Selection** pane, select both **imageRight** and **Myself**.

19. Apply the **Fade** animation to both selected objects.

20. On the Animations tab, select **Animation Pane**.

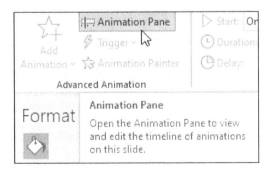

© 2020, IconLogic, Inc. All Rights Reserved.

NOTES

The Animation Pane allows you to see and manage the animations on a selected slide. For instance, you can drag or stretch any of the squares next to each animation to either extend that animation's playtime or delay when the animation occurs.

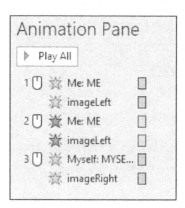
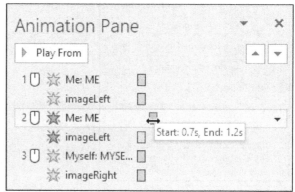

21. On the slide, position the two Samantha images on top of each other similar to what is shown below.

22. From the **iSpring Suite** tab on the Ribbon, Preview the selected slide.

Each time you click the slide, you'll see the fade-in and fade-out animations. After you learn about audio during the next module, you'll be able to synchronize animations like these with audio.

23. Save and close the PowerPoint presentation.

© 2020, IconLogic, Inc. All Rights Reserved.

Backgrounds and Templates

So far you've opened a few existing presentations and then used a combination of PowerPoint and iSpring tools to edit the slides. And during upcoming modules, you'll open other existing presentations and add more and more awesome stuff to them (like audio, videos, quizzes, and interactivity).

Although opening and editing existing content are common tasks, sooner or later you're going to need to create content from scratch. Although creating a new presentation is simple, the presentation needs to look good, provide context and relevance, and have a decent structure. When it comes to the look of a presentation, you can use the PowerPoint **Design** tab on the **Ribbon** to get a nice-looking theme. However, applying a theme does not add any content to your presentation (themes simply change the way existing slides look). It's doubtful that you'll find a theme that adequately represents your industry (for instance, there's no Medical Theme). And themes don't offer suggestions on project structure for your eLearning content (you'll need to add all of the slides and apply slide layouts as appropriate).

You'll find iSpring's Backgrounds and Templates helpful as you kick-start your project. Backgrounds allow you to take any blank slide and enhance it with supplied background images. Templates let you add one or multiple slides to a project that, in addition to containing an assortment of theme-related background images, include helpful text placeholders that suggest content that you might want to incorporate.

Guided Activity 4: Insert a Background

1. Insert a Hospital Background onto a slide.

    ☐ ensure that PowerPoint is open, but all presentations are closed

    ☐ select the **iSpring Suite 9** tab on the Ribbon

    ☐ from the **Content Library** group, click **Backgrounds**

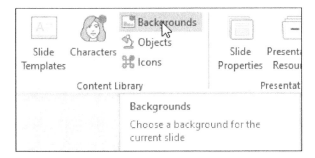

    Because you don't have a presentation open, you are prompted to either open an existing presentation or create a new one.

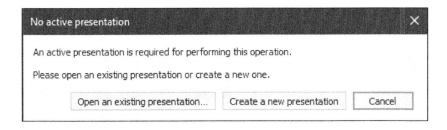

    ☐ click the **Create a new presentation** button

    ☐ from the **Content Library** group, click **Backgrounds** again

© 2020, IconLogic, Inc. All Rights Reserved.

This time the **Backgrounds** dialog box opens.

☐ from the list at the left, select **Hospitals**

☐ select any of the background images

☐ click the **Insert** button

The selected image is added to the presentation and automatically sized to fit perfectly on the slide.

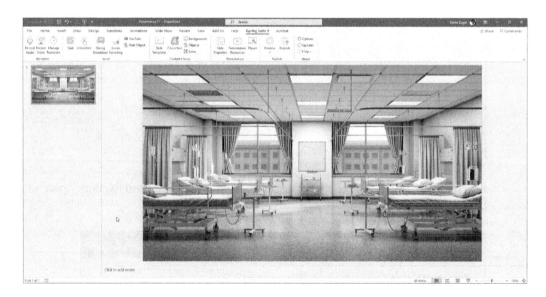

© 2020, IconLogic, Inc. All Rights Reserved.

Backgrounds Confidence Check

1. Insert a Character from the **Medicine** category onto the background. (You learned about Characters on page 26.)

2. Resize and reposition the Character as appropriate to work best with the Background image.

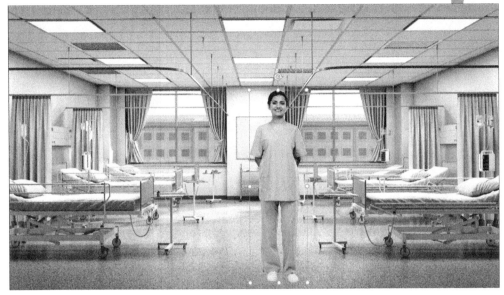

3. Insert a few blank slides into the presentation and then spend a few moments adding backgrounds and characters as appropriate.

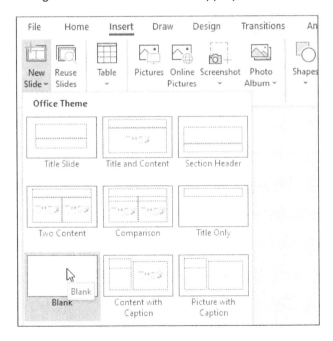

4. When finished, save the presentation to the iSpring9Data folder as **MyScene**.

© 2020, IconLogic, Inc. All Rights Reserved.

Guided Activity 5: Insert Template Slides

1. Ensure that the **MyScene** presentation you created during the last activity is still open.

2. Insert Template slides.

   ❏ select slide **1**

   ❏ from the **iSpring** tab on the **Ribbon**, **Content Library** group, click **Slide Templates**

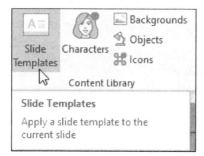

   The Slide Templates dialog box opens.

   ❏ from the **Slide type** list at the left, select **Opening**

   ❏ from the middle of the Slide Templates dialog box, scroll down to the **Hospital Scenario** category

   ❏ select all three slides in the Hospital Scenario group

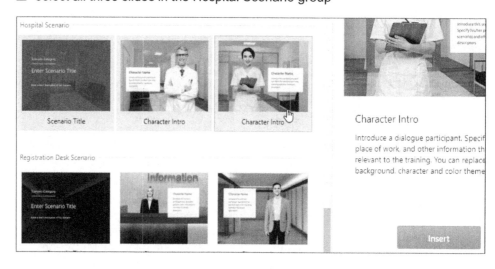

   ❏ click the **Insert** button

   Three slides are added to your presentation.

© 2020, IconLogic, Inc. All Rights Reserved.

Slide Templates Confidence Check

1. Using the PowerPoint Filmstrip, drag the three new slides to the top of the other presentation slides.

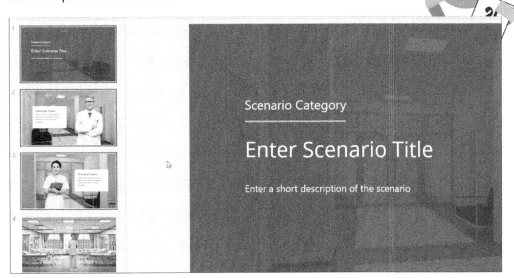

2. On slide 1, edit the placeholder text as shown below.

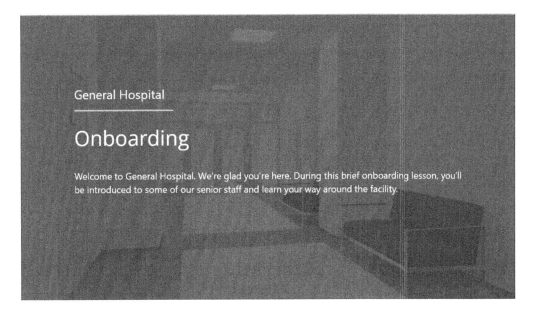

3. On slide 2, edit the placeholder text as shown at the right.

4. Spend a few moments adding some **Content slide types** from the **Hospital Scenario** templates.

5. Save and close the presentation.

NOTES

© 2020, IconLogic, Inc. All Rights Reserved.

Notes

© 2020, IconLogic, Inc. All Rights Reserved.

iCONLOGiC

"Skills and Drills" Learning

Module 2: Working with Voiceover Audio

In This Module You Will Learn About:

And You Will Learn To:

Voiceover Scripts

In my experience, voiceover audio enhances the learner experience, even if the audio isn't perfect. You likely won't have the budget to hire a professional narrator (even though professionals are far less expensive than most people believe), so it's likely up to you to record the audio. Horrors, right? Your voice sounds terrible, right? Perhaps you think the sound of your voice is a cross between Mickey Mouse and Darth Vader? Believe it or not, most people (including you) hate the sound of their own voice. Cut yourself some slack. Your voice is perfect for your corporate eLearning. Rest assured that you do not have to have the voice of a radio talk-show host to record awesome voiceover audio.

Here are four things that you can do to improve your voiceover audio right away:

1. **Write down** exactly what you are going to narrate, slide-by-slide (this kind of narration is often referred to as a voiceover script).

2. Add the voiceover script directly into PowerPoint's **Notes** panel where it will be readily available when it comes to both rehearse and record the audio.

3. **Rehearse** the script prior to recording so that when the time comes to record, you don't sound like you're simply reading a speech.

4. Keep your voiceover audio **short** and sweet. Given how distracted learners can be, the ideal slide playtime, including images, animations, and audio, should be approximately **30 seconds**.

In the activities that follow, you'll learn how to add a voiceover script to PowerPoint's Notes panel. Because you can record audio directly from within iSpring, you'll also learn how to use the Notes as an aid to recording audio.

Guided Activity 6: Add Notes to Serve as Voiceover Audio

1. Using PowerPoint, open the **VoiceoverScriptMe.pptx** file from the iSpring9Data folder.

2. Type voiceover text within PowerPoint's Notes pane.

   ☐ ensure you are working on slide **1** and in **Normal** view

   ☐ below the slide, click on the text that says **Click to add notes**

The placeholder text disappears, and you can now type your own notes.

   ☐ type **This is a Grammar Guide presentation.**

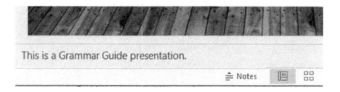

© 2020, IconLogic, Inc. All Rights Reserved.

3. Type more voiceover text within PowerPoint's Notes pane.

    ❏ select slide **2**

    ❏ click within the Notes pane and type: **Welcome to the Grammar Guide. Today's topic is Me, Myself, and I. Wait. That sounded a little self-centered. I mean our topic is how to tell when to use each of these personal pronouns.**

    Welcome to the Grammar Guide. Today's topic is Me, Myself, and I. Wait. That sounded a little self-centered. I mean our topic is how to tell when to use each of these personal pronouns.

4. Copy and paste voiceover text from a Word document into PowerPoint's Notes pane.

    ❏ minimize PowerPoint

    ❏ using Microsoft Word, open **VoiceoverTextForSlides.docx** from the iSpring9Data folder.

    ❏ select the text for slide **3**, not including the heading that says Slide 3

    > **Slide 2**
    > Welcome to the Grammar Guide. Today's topic is Me, Myself, and I. Wait. That sounded a little self-centered. I mean our topic is how to tell when to use each of these personal pronouns.
    >
    > **Slide 3**
    > There are times when the word **myself** has grated on my ear—and I have not known why. The misuse of the pronoun **myself** in certain sentences was one of those things that I knew sounded wrong, but I could not quite explain why.

    ❏ press [**ctrl**] [**c**] to copy the selected text to the clipboard

    ❏ return to PowerPoint (the **VoiceoverScriptMe** presentation should still be open)

    ❏ select slide **3**

    ❏ click within the Notes pane

    ❏ press [**ctrl**] [**v**] to paste the voiceover text into the Notes pane

    There are times when someone's grammar has grated on my ear—and I have not known why. The misuse of the pronoun **myself** in certain sentences was one of those things that I knew sounded wrong, but I could not quite explain why.

5. Save your work.

Voiceover Confidence Check

1. Copy and paste the voiceover text from the Word document to the Notes pane for slides 4, 5, and 6.

    Each slide should now contain voiceover text in their respective Notes pane.

2. Save and close **VoiceoverScriptMe**.

3. Close the Word document (there is no need to save the document if prompted).

© 2020, IconLogic, Inc. All Rights Reserved.

Recording Voiceover Audio

iSpring allows you to record voiceover for each slide—or for a series of slides—without having to leave PowerPoint. You can even synchronize your voiceover with animations on the slide to simulate what you would do in a live classroom.

If you prefer, you can record the voiceover outside of PowerPoint/iSpring by using a sound-recording program such as **Audacity** (https://www.audacityteam.org) or by hiring voiceover talent to do the recording. You can then import the audio into the presentation.

If you plan to record your own audio, you need a microphone connected to your computer. Once you've got the microphone, consider the following:

Setup: If you plan to use high-end audio hardware, such as a mixer or preamplifier, plug your microphone into the hardware and then plug the hardware into your computer's "line in" port. Set the volume on your mixer or preamplifier to just under zero (this will minimize distortion).

Microphone placement: The microphone should be positioned four to six inches from your mouth to reduce the chance that nearby sounds are recorded. Ideally, you should position the microphone above your nose and pointed down at your mouth. Also, if you position the microphone just to the side of your mouth, you can soften the sound of the letters *S* and *P*.

Microphone technique: It's a good idea to keep a glass of water close by and, just before recording, take a drink. To eliminate the annoying breathing and lip smack sounds, turn away from the microphone, take a deep breath, exhale, take another deep breath, open your mouth, turn back toward the microphone, and start speaking. Speak slowly. When recording for the first time, many people race through the content. Recording audio isn't a competitive race to any sort of finish line. *Take your time.*

Guided Activity 7: Record Voiceover Audio

1. Using PowerPoint, open the **RecordAudioMe.pptx** file from the iSpring9Data folder.

   This presentation contains slides with a voiceover script in the Notes area.

2. Run the microphone set-up wizard.

   ☐ from far right of the **iSpring Suite** tab, **About** section, click **Options**

   The Options dialog box opens.

   ☐ from the **Microphone** drop-down menu, ensure the microphone you'd like to use for the recording is selected

   ☐ from the **Volume** area, click **Set up microphone**

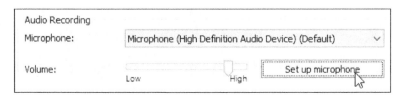

© 2020, IconLogic, Inc. All Rights Reserved.

The Microphone Wizard opens.

☐ work through the wizard as necessary (in particular, you'll be asked to select your microphone from a list and ensure the microphone can hear you)

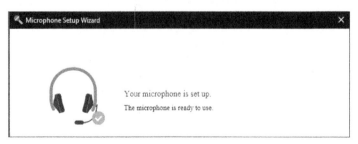

☐ when finished, click the **Finish** button and then click the **OK** button to close the Options dialog box

---

     © 2020, IconLogic, Inc. All Rights Reserved.

3. Record a voiceover for slide 1.

   ❏ select slide **1**

   ❏ from the **iSpring Suite** tab, **Narration** section, click **Record Audio**

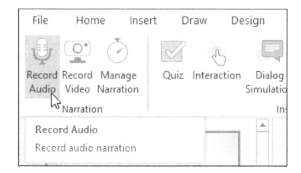

The presentation goes into slideshow view, and the **Record Audio Narration** dialog box opens.

   ❏ if necessary, enable **Show slide notes**

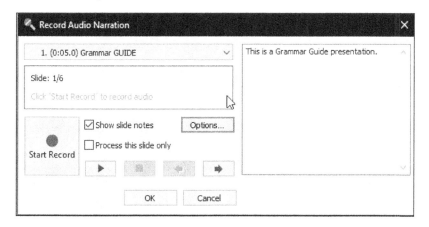

The script you added to the Notes area appears in the panel at the right.

   ❏ click the **Start Record** button

   ❏ read the voiceover script text aloud

   ❏ when finished, click the **Stop** icon

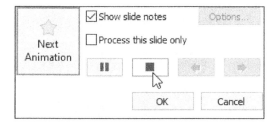

   ❏ click the **OK** button

4. Preview slide **1** to hear the audio that you just recorded.

© 2020, IconLogic, Inc. All Rights Reserved.

5. Close the preview.

   If you are unhappy with your voiceover audio, you can re-record new audio by clicking the **Record Audio** icon again (you'll be prompted to replace the current audio).

6. Record audio for the second slide.

   ❑ select slide **2**

   ❑ from the **iSpring Suite** tab, **Narration** section, click **Record Audio**

   Once again, the presentation goes into slideshow view and the **Record Audio Narration** dialog box opens.

   ❑ click the **Start Record** button

   ❑ read the voiceover script slide 2 aloud

   ❑ when finished, click the **Stop** icon

   ❑ click the **OK** button

7. Preview slide **2** to hear the audio that you just recorded.

8. Close the preview.

   As with slide 1, if you are unhappy with the voiceover that you recorded, you can re-record new audio by clicking the **Record Audio** icon.

9. Save and close the presentation.

© 2020, IconLogic, Inc. All Rights Reserved.

Importing Audio

During the last few activities, you learned how to record voiceover audio directly into iSpring. However, as mentioned earlier, you can record the voiceover outside of iSpring via a sound-recording program or hire voiceover talent to do the recording for you. If you choose either of these routes, the next step is to import the audio into iSpring.

You can import three types of audio files into a iSpring Suite project: WAV, MP3, and WMA.

WAV (WAVE): WAV files are one of the original digital audio standards. This kind of file, although of high quality, can be large (easily a few megabytes of storage per minute of play time). If your learner has a slow Internet connection, the download times for large files can be problematic.

MP3 (MPEG Audio Layer III): MP3 files are compressed digital audio files. File sizes in this format are typically 90 percent smaller than WAV files.

WMA (Windows Media Audio): Although similar to MP3, Microsoft's WMA files can compress at a higher rate so they will typically be smaller (in bytes).

> **Note:** You can learn more about digital audio formats by visiting **www.webopedia.com/DidYouKnow/Computer_Science/2005/ digital_audio_formats.asp** (a site that details common audio formats).

Guided Activity 8: Import and Review an Audio File

1. Using PowerPoint, open **ImportAudioMe.pptx** from the iSpring9Data folder.

   This project consists of 16 slides. Each of the slides contains slide notes but no audio.

2. Import audio for one slide.

   ☐ from the **iSpring Suite** tab, **Narration** section, click **Manage Narration**

   The **iSpring Narration Editor** opens where you can import or record audio and videos, synchronize audio with slide animations, and edit clips.

   ☐ from the **Import** section, click **Audio**

   The Import Audio Clips dialog box opens.

   ☐ navigate to the **iSpring9Data** folder

© 2020, IconLogic, Inc. All Rights Reserved.

NOTES

❏ open the **audio** folder

❏ open **slide1.wav**

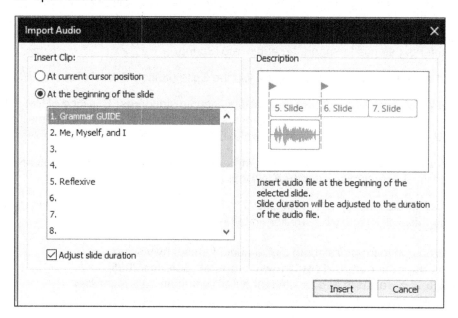

At the left of the dialog box, notice that **Adjust slide duration** is selected by default. iSpring will ensure that the slide stays onscreen long enough for the audio to play. In this case, iSpring will adjust the playtime for slide 1 slightly to accommodate the audio.

❏ click the **Insert** button

The audio is added to the Playback area. You can see blue, squiggly lines known as a **waveform** (a digital representative of the audio file you imported).

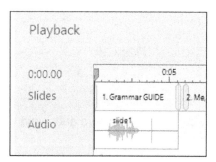

3. Preview the audio.

❏ from the Playback area, click the **Play** button to hear the audio

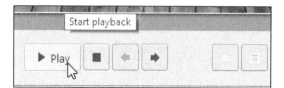

© 2020, IconLogic, Inc. All Rights Reserved.

A thin blue line—the Playhead—progresses across the waveform, and you hear the imported voiceover audio.

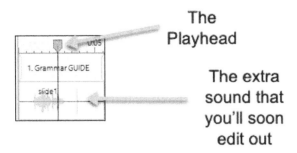

The Playhead

The extra sound that you'll soon edit out

If you listen carefully, you can also hear extra sounds (perhaps a clap and then a faint mouse click). You'll learn to remove these kinds of noises soon.

Since there isn't any audio after the mouse click sound, allowing the Playhead to continue to move doesn't make much sense, so it's time to Pause the playback.

❑ click the **Pause** button

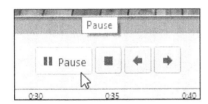

❑ click the **Save & Close** button to close the Manage Narration screen

4. Save the project.

Importing Audio Confidence Check

1. Working within the **ImportAudioMe** project, import **slide2.wav** onto slide 2.

2. Import **slide3.wav** onto slide 3.

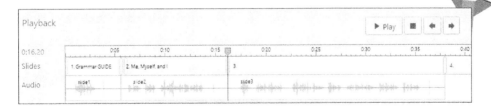

3. Drag the **Playhead** back to the far left of the Playback area and then **Play** the audio that you've just imported.

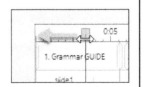

You'll notice that there are plenty of noises between the waves on the waveform that need to be cleaned up. You'll take care of that next.

4. Save and close the project.

NOTES

Editing Audio

In a perfect world, voiceover audio that you record or import into iSpring would be perfect. There wouldn't be noises between the waves of a waveform. There wouldn't be any narrator gaffes to delete and the audio levels from one recording to the next would be consistent. Unfortunately, the world's not perfect, and knowing how to make simple edits to an audio file is a necessity. Although iSpring Suite isn't the most powerful audio editing tool in the world, you'll find that there are enough editing options to allow you to delete unwanted parts of a waveform, add silence, and even control the volume levels across an entire presentation.

Guided Activity 9: Trim Audio

1. Using PowerPoint, open the **EditMyAudio.pptx** file from the iSpring9Data folder.

   This 16-slide presentation is loaded with audio. Much of the audio needs editing.

   ☐ from the **iSpring Suite** tab, **Narration** section, click **Manage Narration**

   The **Manage Narration** screen opens.

   ☐ in the **Playback** area, click to the left of the first audio clip (to move the Playhead to the beginning of the first waveform)

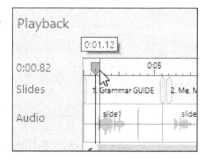

2. Play the audio.

   Near the end of slide 1, unwanted sounds can be heard after the narrator is finished speaking. You'll edit the audio clip next and remove the unwanted sounds.

3. Pause the audio playback.

4. Open the audio editor.

   ☐ in the **Playback** area, click once in the middle of the first audio clip

   The selected clip turns yellow.

   ☐ on the **Home** tab of the Ribbon, **Editing** group, click **Edit Clip**

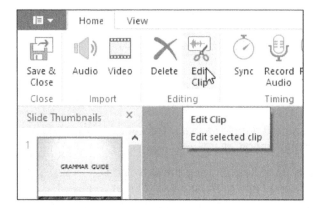

   The audio editor opens.

 © 2020, IconLogic, Inc. All Rights Reserved.

5. Zoom closer to the waveform.

☐ at the **bottom right** of the Audio Editor window, drag the **Zoom** slider **right** to zoom closer to the waveform (if necessary)

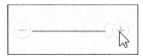

☐ highlight the area of the waveform shown below (this is the portion of the waveform that contains the two audio gaffes that need to be removed)

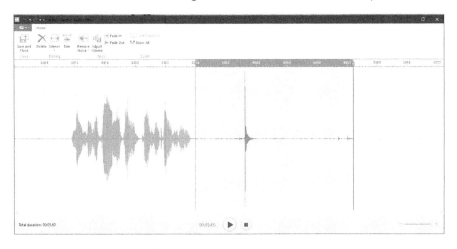

☐ press the **Play** button to listen to just the selected portion of the audio clip

Now that you've isolated and listened the problem area of the audio clip, you're ready to trim the audio. But stop for a moment. I asked you to highlight the portion of the audio shown in the image above so you could confirm the unwanted audio in the clip was located. To trim audio, you first select the portion of the audio you want to keep and then trim. If you've edited audio in other programs, it's possible that selecting a portion of the audio you want to keep is the reverse of what you normally do. (In other programs, you would select the unwanted portion of the audio clip and delete/trim it.)

☐ select the portion of the audio clip *that you want to keep* (similar to what is shown in the image below)

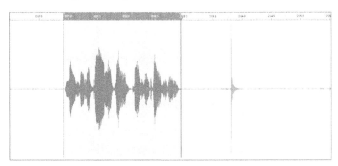

NOTES

© 2020, IconLogic, Inc. All Rights Reserved.

❏ from the **Home** tab on the Ribbon, **Editing** group, click **Trim**

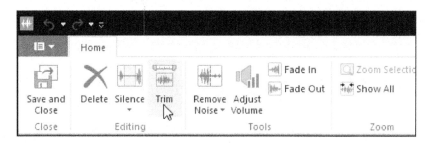

The selected portion of the audio clip is retained, the unselected portion is deleted.

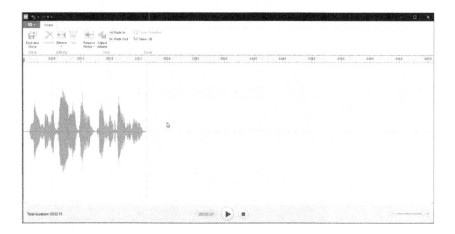

❏ from the top of the Ribbon, click **Save and Close**

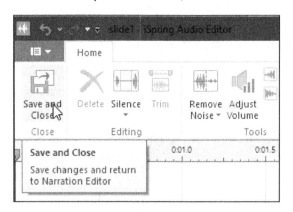

You are returned to the **Manage Narration** screen.

6. Ensure the **Playhead** is at the beginning of the **Playback** area.

7. Click the **Play** button.

The edited audio clip is cleaner and shorter. However, by shortening the clip, you've introduced a new problem. There is too much time between the end of the audio on the first slide, the end of the slide, and the appearance of the next slide. You'll fix the timing problem next.

© 2020, IconLogic, Inc. All Rights Reserved.

Guided Activity 10: Change Slide Timing

1. Ensure that the **EditMyAudio.pptx** presentation is still open and that you're on the Manage Narration screen.

2. Shorten the Playtime for a slide.

   ☐ in the **Playback** area, drag the second yellow icon left

   As you drag the icon, notice that all of the icons and clips to the right move left and get closer to the first audio clip.

   ☐ position the yellow icon approximately an eighth of an inch away from the first clip (if you move the icon too close to the first clip, you'll jump from slide one to slide two a bit too quickly)

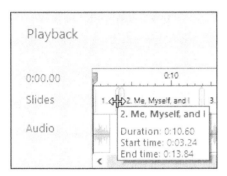

3. Ensure the **Playhead** is at the beginning of the Playback area.

4. Click the **Play** button.

   The transition from slide one to slide two should be much better.

© 2020, IconLogic, Inc. All Rights Reserved.

Guided Activity 11: Silence Audio

1. Ensure that the **EditMyAudio.pptx** presentation is still open and that you're on the Manage Narration screen.

2. From the Slide Thumbnails at the left of the Manage Narration screen, select slide **7**.

   The Playhead automatically moves to slide 7 in the Playback area.

3. Click the **Play** button.

   If you listen carefully, there is a faint sound between the sentences "Is myself correct? Or should the word be... ," specifically after the word "correct." You'd like to remove the sound, but if you trim the audio like you learned how to do earlier, the timing between the two sentences will be shortened and ultimately be a bit too fast. This is the perfect place to use iSpring's Silence audio feature where you can remove unwanted audio without changing the length of an audio clip.

4. Silence audio.

   ☐ in the **Playback** area, click once in the middle of the seventh audio clip

   The selected clip turns yellow.

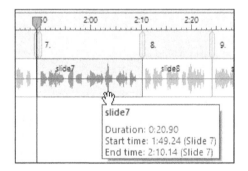

   ☐ on the **Home** tab of the Ribbon, **Editing** group, click **Edit Clip**

   ☐ highlight the unwanted sound (it's between seconds **9** and **10** and is shown selected in the image below)

© 2020, IconLogic, Inc. All Rights Reserved.

☐ from the **Home** tab on the Ribbon, **Editing** group, click **Silence**

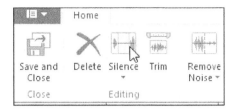

The selected portion of the audio clip is removed, but the length of the audio clip did not change.

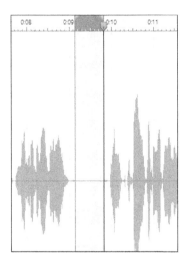

5. Click the **Play** button to confirm that the sound has, in fact, been silenced.

6. From the Ribbon, click **Save and Close**.

7. On the Manage Narration screen, click **Save and Close** to return to PowerPoint and iSpring.

8. Save the presentation.

Guided Activity 12: Adjust Audio Volume

1. Ensure that the **EditMyAudio** project is still open.

2. Open the Manage Narration screen.

3. From the Slide Thumbnails at the left of the Manage Narration screen, select slide **5**.

4. Position the Playhead approximately half-way through slide 5.

5. Click the **Play** button.

   The audio level for the slide is fine. However, when you get to slide 6, you'll notice that the volume for the audio on slide 6 is much louder than the audio on slide 5. You'll attempt to fix the problem by lowering the volume on slide 6.

6. Click the **Pause** button.

7. Lower the volume of selected audio.

   ☐ select the audio clip for slide **6**

   ☐ on the **Home** tab of the Ribbon, **Editing** group, click **Edit Clip**

   ☐ click in the middle of the clip and press [**ctrl**] [**a**] on your keyboard to select the entire clip

   ☐ from the **Home** tab on the Ribbon, **Editing** group, click **Adjust volume**

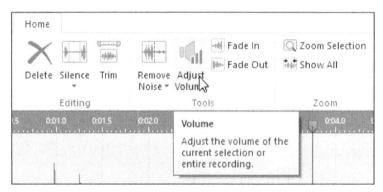

   The Adjust Volume dialog box opens.

   ☐ drag the slider **left** to lower the volume of the clip by approximately **20%**

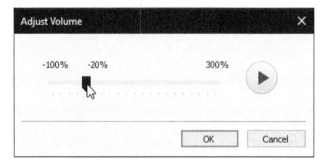

   ☐ click the **OK** button

　　　　　　　　© 2020, IconLogic, Inc. All Rights Reserved.

8. From the Ribbon, click **Save and Close** to return to the Manage Narration screen.

9. Position the Playhead approximately half-way through slide 5.

10. Click the **Play** button.

   Because you lowered the volume for the slide 6 audio, the height of the waveform for slide 6 has gotten shorter. Generally speaking, the shorter a waveform, the lower the volume. Although the waveform for slide 6 is still a bit taller than the waveform for slide 5, the difference in the volume between the two slides has been minimized.

11. Click the **Pause** button.

Audio Editing Confidence Check

1. Go through the audio on all of the slides and trim the unwanted audio (you should easily be able to identify the unwanted audio) or add silence as appropriate.

2. Spend a few moments raising or lowering the volume of the audio throughout the presentation until the levels sound consistent to you.

3. Adjust the timing for each of the slides as appropriate.

4. Save and close the presentation.

Notes

© 2020, IconLogic, Inc. All Rights Reserved.

iCONLOGiC

"Skills and Drills" Learning

Module 3: Videos, Pictures, and Syncing Animations

In This Module You Will Learn About:

And You Will Learn To:

Videos

iSpring Suite supports several types of video formats including avi, mkv, mp4, mpg, and wmv. If your computer setup includes a video camera, you can also record your own video. When adding videos to a presentation, you can elect to import the video directly onto a slide or have the video appear on the sidebar. If you want the video to appear directly on a slide, you use PowerPoint's video handling capabilities. If you want the video to appear on the sidebar (as shown circled in the image below), you use iSpring's **Manage Narration** dialog box and, using the Player dialog box, enable the sidebar.

Guided Activity 13: Add a Video to the Sidebar

1. Using PowerPoint, open **VideoImageMe.pptx**.

2. Import a video and use it in the sidebar.

   ☐ from the **iSpring Suite** tab, **Narration** section, click **Manage Narration**

   ☐ from the **Slide Thumbnails**, select **slide 1**

   ☐ click the **Home** tab on the Ribbon and, from the **Import** group, click **Video**

   ☐ from **iSpring9Data** folder, open the **Images_Videos** folder

   ☐ open **Safety_Intro.mp4**

 © 2020, IconLogic, Inc. All Rights Reserved.

The Import Video dialog box opens. From here, you can decide when the video appears.

❏ from the **Insert Clip** area, select **At the beginning of the slide** (if necessary)

❏ ensure **1. Welcome** is selected

❏ from the bottom of the dialog box, ensure **Adjust slide duration** is selected (this will ensure that if a long video is added to the slide, the slide will remain onscreen long enough for the video to complete)

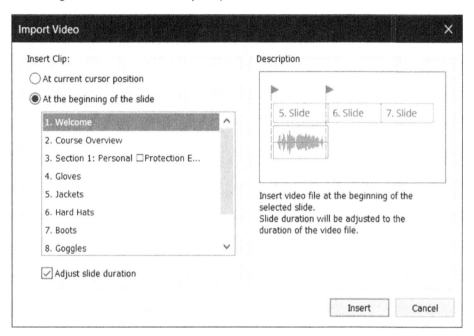

❏ click the **Insert** button

The video appears in the Playback area (in the Video channel) and to the right of the slide.

Does it seem odd that the video is currently positioned to the right of the slide instead of directly on the slide? In reality, the video is not on the slide at all but has automatically been added to the **sidebar** (which you'll learn about next).

© 2020, IconLogic, Inc. All Rights Reserved.

3. Click the **Save and Close** button to close the Manage Audio dialog box.

4. Enable the Sidebar.

    ☐ from the **iSpring Suite** tab, **Presentation** group, click **Player**

The Customize Player dialog box opens. This dialog box allows you to enable the Sidebar, a Notes area, and more. You'll visit this dialog box multiple times over the course of this book. For now, you're looking only to enable the Sidebar.

    ☐ from the **Layout** area at the left, select **Sidebar**

    ☐ from the **Location** drop-down menu, ensure **On the left** is selected

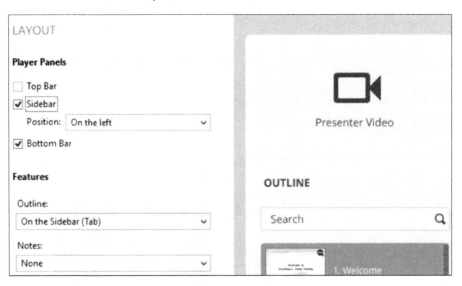

    ☐ from the **Close** area, click **Apply & Close**

© 2020, IconLogic, Inc. All Rights Reserved.

5. Preview the first slide to see both the Sidebar and the video (the Sidebar is indicated by the arrow in the image below).

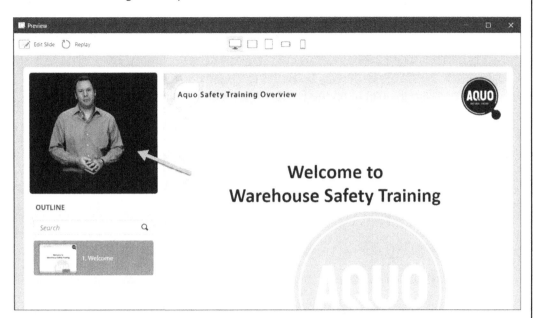

6. Close the preview window.

7. Save your work.

© 2020, IconLogic, Inc. All Rights Reserved.

Guided Activity 14: Insert a Video onto a Slide

1. Ensure that the **VideoImageMe.pptx** is still open.

2. Add a video onto a slide.

   ☐ select slide **4**

   ☐ from the **Insert** tab on the Ribbon, **Media** group, click **Video** and choose **Video on My PC**

   The Video dialog box opens.

   ☐ from **iSpring9Data** folder, open the **Images_Videos** folder

   ☐ open **gloves.mp4**

   The video is added to the middle of the slide.

3. Resize and position video on a slide.

   ☐ drag the video until its left edge is a few pixels from the upper left edge of the green rectangle

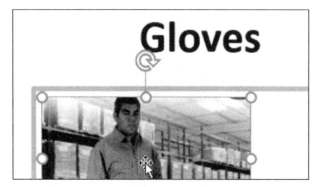

   Note: By default, PowerPoint's **Snap to Grid** feature is enabled, making it a bit frustrating to position objects exactly where you'd like. To temporarily disable the Snap to Grid feature, press [**alt**] while you position the video. As long as you keep the [**alt**] key pressed, you'll be able to control the video's slide position. To disable the Snap to Grid feature, click the **View** tab in the Ribbon and, in the **Show** group, click the icon on the bottom right corner of the group to open the Grids and Guides dialog box. Deselect **Snap objects to grid** and then click the **OK** button.

© 2020, IconLogic, Inc. All Rights Reserved.

❑ drag the lower right corner resizing handle down and to the right so that the video fits nicely inside the rectangle

4. Using the **iSpring Suite** tab on the Ribbon, **Preview** slide **4**.

   The video does not play automatically. Click the video to get it to play. (You'll get the videos to play automatically when you learn to synchronize animations, which you'll do shortly.)

5. Close the Preview.

6. Save your work.

Pictures

You can import several graphic formats onto a PowerPoint slide including, but not limited to, BMPs (Windows Bitmap), GIFs (Graphics Interchange Format), JPG or JPEG (Joint Photographic Expert Group), WMFs (MetaFiles), and PNGs (Portable Network Graphics).

Once the image has been imported onto a slide, it can be manipulated like any PowerPoint image (you can resize images, crop them, group them, animate them, re-color them, etc.).

Guided Activity 15: Insert a Picture onto a Slide

1. Ensure that the **VideoImageMe.pptx** is still open.

2. Add an image to slide 2.

   ☐ select slide **2** and, from the PowerPoint Ribbon, **Insert** tab, **Images** group, and click **Pictures**

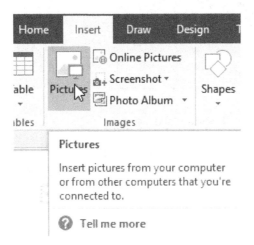

   ☐ from the **iSpring9Data** folder, open the **Images_Videos** folder
   ☐ open **PPE.png**

3. Drag the image to the left of the slide.

© 2020, IconLogic, Inc. All Rights Reserved.

Images and Videos Confidence Check

1. Still working within the **VideoImageMe.pptx** project, insert the following three pictures onto slide **2**:

   ShopSafety.png

   WarehouseSafety.png

   PreventiveSafety.png

2. Position the four images on the slide similar to the picture shown below.

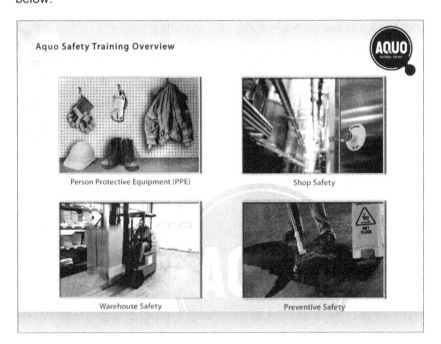

3. On slide **5**, insert the **shirt** video.

4. Resize and reposition the video with the green rectangle.

5. On slide **6**, insert the **hardhat** video.

6. Resize and reposition the video with the green rectangle.

7. On slide **7**, insert the **boots** video.

8. Resize and reposition the video with the green rectangle.

9. On slide **8**, insert the **goggles** video.

10. Resize and reposition the video with the green rectangle.

11. On slide **9**, add the **Safety_Outro** video to the **Sidebar**.

12. Using the **iSpring Suite** tab, **Preview** the entire presentation to view the videos and images you've imported during this module.

13. Close the Preview.

14. Save and close the presentation.

NOTES

© 2020, IconLogic, Inc. All Rights Reserved.

Syncing

During the past few activities, you've learned to add both images and videos to a PowerPoint presentation/iSpring eLearning course. And during other lessons, you've learned to add audio. But adding images, audio, text, shapes, and videos, is just the beginning. You can animate just about anything in PowerPoint. After you've added the animations, you can use iSpring to control when the animations occur, object by object and slide by slide.

Guided Activity 16: Animate a Slide Object

1. Using PowerPoint, open **SynchMe.pptx**.

2. Using the **iSpring Suite** tab on the Ribbon, Preview **slide 1**.

    Notice that there is an orange callout on the slide. It's a helpful reminder to learners that they can move from slide to slide by using the green navigation buttons.

You're going to do two things with the callout. First, you're going to animate it have it Fade in on the slide. Second, you'll control when the callout appears onscreen by using iSpring Suite's synchronization capabilities.

3. Close the Preview.

© 2020, IconLogic, Inc. All Rights Reserved.

4. Animate the callout.

   ❑ on slide **1**, select the **orange callout**

   ❑ from the **Animations** tab on the Ribbon, **Animation** group, click **Fade**

   ❑ from the **Animations** tab on the Ribbon, **Advanced Animation** group, click **Animation Pane**

The animation you added to the orange callout appears on the Animation Pane. Notice from the Timing area of the Animations tab that the animation is set to Start On Click with no delay.

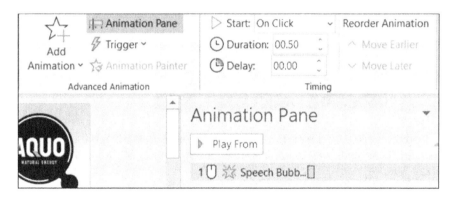

5. Using the **iSpring Suite** tab on the Ribbon, Preview **slide 1**.

   Now that you've added an animation to the callout, you're required to click the slide to see the callout fade and the Sidebar video. In the next activity, you'll use iSpring to delay when the callout appears onscreen. Specifically, the appearance of the callout will be delayed until *after* the video is finished.

6. Close the Preview.

Guided Activity 17: Synchronize Animations

1. Ensure that the **SynchMe.pptx** presentation is still open.

2. Synchronize an animation with voiceover audio.

   ❑ from the **iSpring Suite** tab, **Narration** section, click **Manage Narration**

   In the Playback area for slide 1, notice that there is a yellow icon (shown circled in the image below). The yellow icon represents the animation that you added to the slide object during the last activity. The icon is currently positioned at 0:00 on the Playback Timeline so the animation occurs immediately.

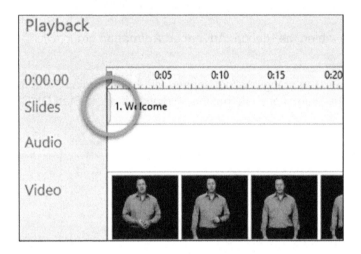

   You can drag the yellow icon along the Playback area to delay when the animation occurs. However, another way to control when an animation occurs is by using iSpring's Synchronize feature.

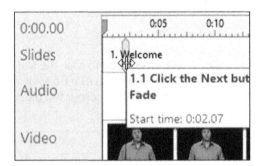

   ❑ from the **Home** tab on the Ribbon, **Timing** group, click **Sync**

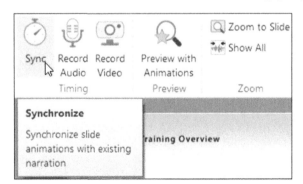

© 2020, IconLogic, Inc. All Rights Reserved.

❑ from the **Synchronize** area, click **Process current slide only**

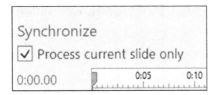

As I've synchronized animations, I've found it helpful to always use **Process current slide only**. Without this option, you'll need to be on your toes and start and stop the process constantly. By Synchronizing one slide at a time, there's less clicking required.

❑ click **Start Sync**

The Playhead begins to move along the Timeline and, as the slide plays, the animation icon is pushed right. It will continue to move right until you click the Stop icon on the toolbar.

❑ click the **Next Animation** button just as the narrator is heard telling learners to "click Next"

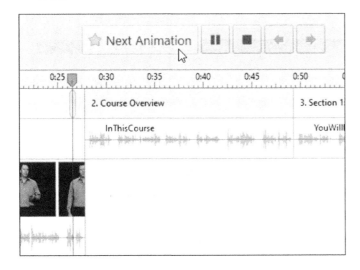

❑ a few seconds after that, click the **Stop** button

If it took you a few seconds to click the Stop button and the timing for slide 1 extended too far right, you can drag the vertical line between slides **left** to **shorten** its playtime.

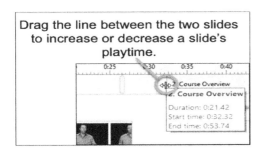

© 2020, IconLogic, Inc. All Rights Reserved.

3. Preview the animation.

☐ from the **Home** tab on the Ribbon, **Preview** group, click **Preview with Animations**

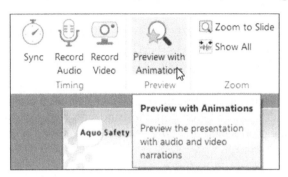

☐ after the callout appears on screen, click the **Exit** button to stop the Preview

4. Save and close the **Manage Narration** screen.

5. On the iSpring Suite tab on the Ribbon, preview slide 1 to see the video positioned on the Sidebar. The animated callout should appear perfectly in sync with the narrator indicating the Next button.

6. Close the preview.

© 2020, IconLogic, Inc. All Rights Reserved.

Synchronization Confidence Check

1. On slide **2**, add a **Fade** animation to each of the four pictures (add the animations one at a time, working from left to right).

2. Use the **Manage Narration** screen to synchronize the audio on slide **2** with the Fade appearance of each image.

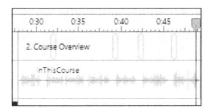

3. **Preview with Animations** and adjust the timing of the animations and slide as necessary.

4. When satisfied, save and close the Manage Narration screen.

5. On slide **3**, add a **Fade** animation to the orange callout.

6. Sync the appearance of the slide 3 callout so that it appears just as the narrator finishes speaking.

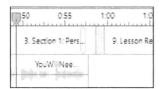

7. Continue using the Sync feature to get the videos on slides 4, 5, 6, 7, and 8 to play as soon as each slide appears.

8. **Preview with Animations** and adjust the timing of the animations and slide as necessary.

9. Save and close the presentation.

Notes

© 2020, IconLogic, Inc. All Rights Reserved.

iCONLOGiC

"Skills and Drills" Learning

Module 4: Interactivity and Screen Recordings

In This Module You Will Learn About:

And You Will Learn To:

Interactions

Interactions, also referred to as iSpring Visuals, allow you to quickly insert interactive objects onto a slide. iSpring Suite comes with a wide range of Interactions that can display information in Pyramids, in Glossaries, or as Processes.

Guided Activity 18: Insert a Labeled Graphic Interaction

1. Using PowerPoint, open the **InteractMe.pptx** file from the **iSpring9Data** folder.

2. Create a Labeled Hotspot interaction on slide 3.

   ☐ select slide **3**

   ☐ from the **iSpring Suite** tab on the Ribbon, **Insert** group, click **Interaction**

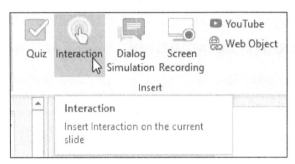

iSpring Visuals opens.

   ☐ from the Create area, click **New Interaction**

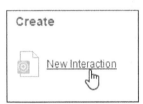

The New Interaction dialog box opens.

   ☐ from the **Annotation** group, select the **Labeled Graphic** interaction

   ☐ click the **Create Interaction** button

The editing window opens.

© 2020, IconLogic, Inc. All Rights Reserved.

3. Replace the background image.

❏ at the right of the editing window, click the **Change** button and choose **From File**

❏ from the **iSpring9Data** folder, open **Images_Videos**

❏ open **PPE.png**

The new image replaces the placeholder image at the right.

4. Edit the interaction's Title.

❏ from the **Labeled Graphic** tab, **Interaction** group, click **Properties**

The **Customization** dialog box opens.

© 2020, IconLogic, Inc. All Rights Reserved.

NOTES

❒ from the Interaction Properties area, change the Title to **Section 1: Personal Protective Equipment (PPEs)**

❒ click the **Apply & Close button**

You'll see the title that you just edited at the top of the interaction once you've finished setting it up, and you see it on the slide.

5. Edit a Label and Description.

❒ from the list at the left, select **Label 1**

❒ change the Label 1 placeholder text to **Gloves**

❒ change the Description placeholder to **Wearing gloves prevents the largest number of industrial accidents.**

6. Change the location of the Gloves hotspot.

❒ from the preview at the right, drag the white dot (this is the **Gloves** hotspot) down until it is optically centered over the gloves image

7. Edit another Label and Description.

❒ from the list at the left, select **Label 2**

© 2020, IconLogic, Inc. All Rights Reserved.

❑ change the Label 1 placeholder text to **Goggles**

❑ change the Description placeholder to **Protection for the eyes.**

8. Change the location of the Goggles hotspot.

   ❑ from the preview at the right, drag the white dot (this is the **Goggles** hotspot and it's currently positioned over the image of the boots) up until it is optically centered over the goggles image

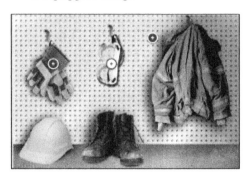

   ❑ from the **Labeled Graphic** tab, **Save** group, click **Save and Return to Course**

The interaction has been added to slide 3.

9. Using the **iSpring Suite** tab on the Ribbon, Preview the Entire Presentation

   When you get to slide **3**, you'll be able to interact with all three of the hotspots (two of the three have been edited; the third hotspot still contains placeholder text).

10. Close the preview.

© 2020, IconLogic, Inc. All Rights Reserved.

Interaction Confidence Check

1. From the **iSpring Suite** tab on the Ribbon, **Insert** group, click **Interaction**.

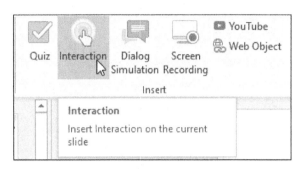

The current slide's interaction opens for editing.

2. Edit the third label as shown in the images below (position the hotspot over the image of the jacket).

3. Add two new labels.

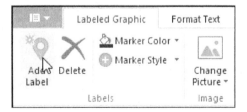

© 2020, IconLogic, Inc. All Rights Reserved.

4. Edit the two new labels as shown in the images below.

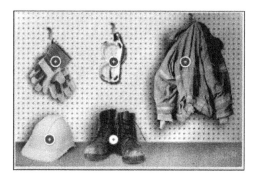

Hardhats

Protection for the head.

Boots

Protection for the feet.

5. Position each of the new hotspots over the appropriate part of the image.

6. Save the interaction and return to the course.

7. Preview the Entire Presentation and, on slide **3**, interact with the hotspots.

8. Close the preview.

9. Save and close the presentation.

© 2020, IconLogic, Inc. All Rights Reserved.

Dialog Simulations

Dialog Simulations combine the concept of Characters (page 26) and Backgrounds (page 33), but take both to a new level. Generally speaking, in a Dialog Simulation you create scenes with one or more clickable items. Depending upon what the learner clicks, they'll jump to a different scene. During the activities that follow, you'll create a medical scenario that will help you determine which lab tests to run when presented with a patient displaying specific symptoms.

Guided Activity 19: Create a Dialog Simulation

1. Create a **new, blank** PowerPoint presentation.

2. Save the presentation to the **iSpring9Data** folder as **MyDialogSimulation**

3. Create a New Simulation.

   ☐ from the **iSpring Suite** tab on the Ribbon, **Insert** group, click **Dialog Simulation**

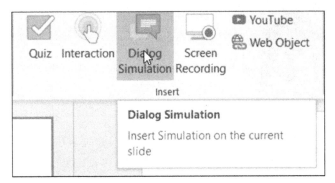

iSpring Talkmaster opens.

   ☐ from the Create area, click **New Simulation**

4. Create a New Scene.

   ☐ on the **Home** tab of the Ribbon, **Scenes** group, click **New Scene**

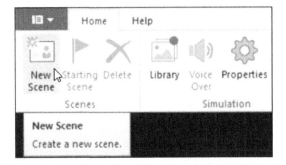

   © 2020, IconLogic, Inc. All Rights Reserved.

☐ on the **Content** tab, type **The lab has been asked to run some tests on a male patient, age 78 years, with anemia. The patient is running a fever of 101 degrees. He is complaining of pain from his abdomen.**

5. Add a Reply.

☐ click **Add replies**

☐ click **Add reply**

The Reply options open.

☐ type **Continue** into the field

☐ click the **Close** button

The Scene you created is the only one in the project. As you move forward, you'll create more scenes, add images, and then link the scenes together. (The scene has two icons at the top left, an alert triangle, and a white flag. The alert icon indicates that you have not yet linked the scene to another scene. The white flag indicates that this scene is the Starting scene (the scene that will be seen first by learners).

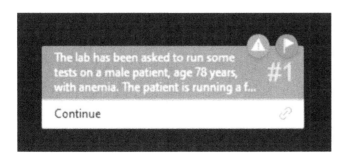

6. Add another scene.

    ☐ on the **Home** tab of the Ribbon, **Scenes** group, click **New Scene**

    ☐ on the **Content** tab, type **Which of these blood tests would you expect to run for this patient?**

7. Add multiple Replies.

    ☐ click **Add replies**

    ☐ click **Add reply**

    ☐ type **HCG**

    ☐ click **Add reply**

    ☐ type **Hematocrit only**

    ☐ click **Add reply**

    ☐ type **CBC**

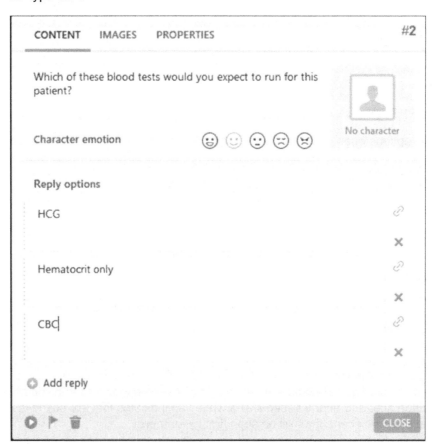

    ☐ click the **Close** button

    The two scenes are stacked on top of each other.

© 2020, IconLogic, Inc. All Rights Reserved.

8. Drag the two scenes away from each other.

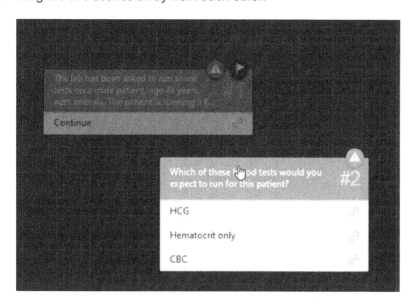

9. Return to the PowerPoint presentation.

   ❏ from the Ribbon, click **Save and Return to Course**

The Dialog Simulation is displayed on the presentation slide.

10. Open the simulation for editing.

    ❏ from the **iSpring Suite** tab on the Ribbon, **Insert** group, click **Dialog Simulation**

© 2020, IconLogic, Inc. All Rights Reserved.

NOTES

Scenes Confidence Check

1. Create a new scene with this Content: **CBC—a Complete Blood Count—is the best answer. This will include counts of the white blood cells, red blood cells, and platelets. It also includes the MCV, hematocrit, MCH, and several other measures.**

2. Add just one reply: **Continue**.

3. Create a new scene with this Content: **Well, hematocrit will give you some of what you want, but it will not include the white blood cell count and some of the other measures you need.**

4. Add just one reply: **Try again!**

5. Create a new scene with this Content: **Wait! That can't be it. That would be a pregnancy test!**

6. Add just one reply: **Try again!**

7. Create a new scene with this Content: **Thanks for working through this scenario. This concludes the lesson.**

8. Add just one reply: **Repeat the lesson**

9. Position the scenes similar to the image below:

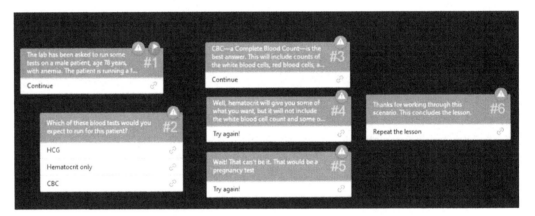

10. Save and close the presentation.

© 2020, IconLogic, Inc. All Rights Reserved.

Guided Activity 20: Link Scenes

1. Using PowerPoint, open the **LinkMe.pptx** file from the **iSpring9Data** folder.

2. Open the simulation for editing.

   ☐ ensure that the presentation's only slide is selected

   ☐ from the **iSpring Suite** tab on the Ribbon, **Insert** group, click **Dialog Simulation**

   ☐ If necessary, drag the stage until the project's six scenes are visible on your screen

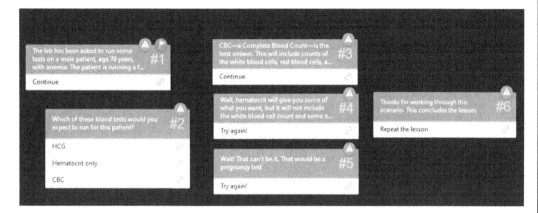

3. Link scene 1 to scene 2.

   ☐ on scene **1**, drag the **link symbol** next to the only reply (shown circled below) in the lower right of the scene to anywhere on scene **2**

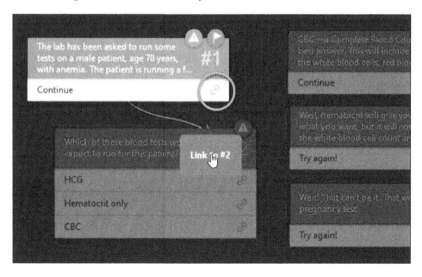

The resulting blue line between two scenes represents the link.

© 2020, IconLogic, Inc. All Rights Reserved.

Linking Scenes Confidence Check

1. From scene **2**, drag the link to **HCG** to scene **5**.

2. From scene **2**, drag the link to **Hematocrit** to scene **4**.

3. From scene **2**, drag the link to **CBC** to scene **3**.

4. CBC is the correct answer. From scene **3**, drag the link to scene **6**.

5. Scene 4 is not a correct answer. From scene **4**, drag the link to scene **2**.

6. Scene 5 is not a correct answer. From scene **5**, drag the link to scene **2**.

7. From scene **6**, drag the link to scene **1**.

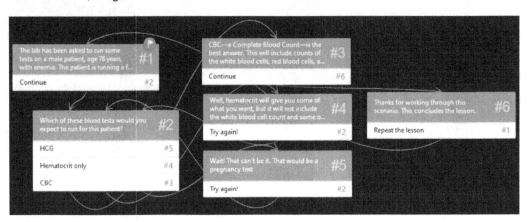

8. Save and return to the course.

9. Preview the presentation and work through the scenario.

10. When finished, close the preview. (Leave the presentation open for the next activity.)

© 2020, IconLogic, Inc. All Rights Reserved.

Guided Activity 21: Add Images to Scenes

1. Using PowerPoint, open the **LinkMe.pptx** file from the **iSpring9Data** folder.

2. Open the simulation for editing.

3. Add a character and a background to scene 1.

   ☐ double-click scene 1 to open it for editing

   ☐ select the **Images** tab

   ☐ click in the middle of the **Background** placeholder

   ☐ scroll through the **Built-In** backgrounds and select the hospital room

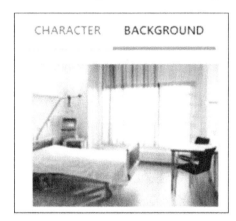

   ☐ to the left of **Background**, click **Character**

   ☐ scroll through the collection of **Characters** and select the **female nurse**

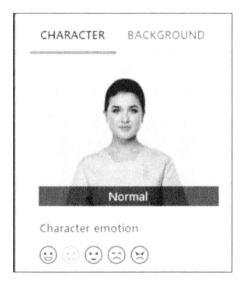

   ☐ from the Character emotion area, ensure Normal is selected (it's the second emotion)

   ☐ click the Close buttons as necessary to dismiss all of the dialog boxes

Linking Scenes Confidence Check

1. Preview the course to see the images you've added to the first scene.

   Because scene 1 is the **Starting scene**, (as denoted by the red flag icon), the images added to the scene are used throughout the project.

2. Close the preview.

3. Open scene **3**.

   Because this scene shows the correct answer, anyone clicking CBC from the previous scene should see a smiley face.

4. On the **Content** tab for scene **3**, click the **first Character emotion**.

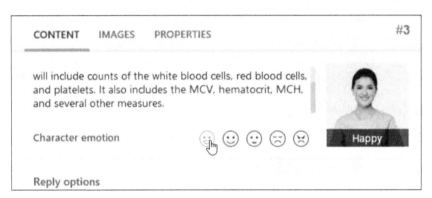

5. Click the **Close** button.

6. Preview the course and, on scene **2**, click **CBC**.

   When scene 3 opens, the nurse is happy with your reply. There is also an emotion meter on the slide. You can easily remove it.

7. Close the preview.

8. Still working in the Simulation, from the **Home** tab, **Simulation** group. click **Player**. Remove the check mark from **Show emotion meter** and then click **Apply & Close**.

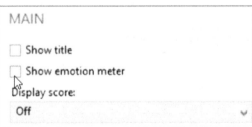

9. Add different emotion icons to the remaining scenes. (Because the remaining replies on scene 2 are incorrect, **Puzzled** or **Unhappy** would be good emotions to use.)

10. When finished, Save and Return to the Course.

11. Save and close the presentation.

© 2020, IconLogic, Inc. All Rights Reserved.

Screen Recordings

Typical iSpring projects consist of individual PowerPoint slides. If you need to demonstrate how to use a software application, you can use any one of several programs to create images of the software. For instance, I used TechSmith SnagIt (**www.snagit.com**) to create the screen captures seen throughout this book. Individual screen captures can then be inserted onto any PowerPoint slide as an image.

As an alternative to using a third-party application to create screen captures, you can use iSpring Suite to record just about anything you can do on your computer. When the recording process is finished, you end up with a single video demonstrating everything you have done during the recording process. A video recording is ideal if you are trying to create an eLearning lesson demonstrating complex mouse actions (like those that would be required when drawing a shape in an image-editing application).

During the next few activities, you'll create a Screen Recording with iSpring Suite. Here's the scenario: you have been hired to create an eLearning course that teaches new employees at your company how to use Notepad. One of the lessons you plan to record includes how to change the page orientation within Notepad.

You could start iSpring's Recorder (iSpring Cam Pro) and click through a process on the fly. However, I've had the best luck with my recordings when I write out the exact steps I'm going to record (this is known as a script) and then rehearse the steps a few times.

Guided Activity 22: Review a Recording Script

Here is a sample script showing the kind of detailed, step-by-step instructions you need to create or receive from a Subject Matter Expert (SME). You are expected to perform each step written below in Notepad.

> Dear iSpring developer, using Notepad, record the process of changing the Page Orientation from Portrait to Landscape, and then back again (from Landscape to Portrait). Create the recording using a capture size of 1280 x 720. Thanks. Your pal, the Subject Matter Expert.

1. Create a new Notepad document.

2. Start the recorder and then, in Notepad, click the **File** menu.

3. Click the **Page Setup** menu item.

4. Click the **Landscape** orientation button.

5. Click the **OK** button.

6. Click the **File** menu.

7. Click the **Page Setup** menu item.

8. Click the **Portrait** orientation button.

9. Click the **OK** button.

10. Stop the recording process.

The script sounds simple. However, you will not know what kind of challenges you might come across unless you rehearse the script prior to recording with iSpring Cam Pro. Let's hold a rehearsal, just as if you were a big-time movie director and you were in charge of a blockbuster movie.

© 2020, IconLogic, Inc. All Rights Reserved.

Guided Activity 23: Rehearse a Script

1. Minimize (hide) PowerPoint.

2. Start Notepad. (Notepad is a standard Windows utility and can be easily accessed via the Window's Start menu or by using Search.)

3. Rehearse the script.

   ☐ using Notepad, click the **File** menu

   ☐ click the **Page Setup** menu item

   ☐ from the **Orientation** area, click **Landscape**

   ☐ click the **OK** button

   ☐ click the **File** menu

   ☐ click the **Page Setup** menu item

   ☐ click the **Portrait** orientation button

   ☐ click the **OK** button

   Hey, look at that! The script worked perfectly... no surprises. You are now ready to work the exact steps again. Only this time, you will record every click that you make. During the recording process, iSpring Cam Pro creates one seamless video as you move through the script.

© 2020, IconLogic, Inc. All Rights Reserved.

Guided Activity 24: Create a Screen Recording

1. Create a **new, blank** PowerPoint presentation.

2. Save the presentation to the **iSpring9Data** folder as **MyScreenRecording**.

3. Create a Screen Recording.

    ❏ from the **iSpring Suite** tab on the Ribbon, **Insert** group, click **Screen Recording**

    iSpring Cam Pro opens.

    ❏ from the **Create** area, click **New Recording**

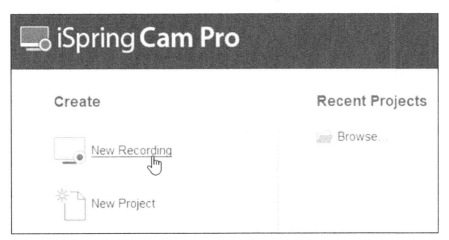

The recording area is the rectangle shape with the dashed lines. Everything within the dashed lines will be recorded. There's also a Recording Settings area where you can control what is recorded, what the size of the capture window is, and if you'll include voiceover audio.

    ❏ from the **Recording Settings** area, select **Screen**

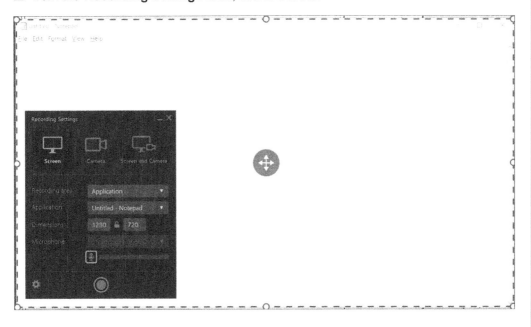

© 2020, IconLogic, Inc. All Rights Reserved.

❏ from the **Recording** area drop-down menu, choose **Application**

❏ from the **Application** area drop-down menu, choose **Untitled Notepad**

❏ from the **Dimensions** area, change the width to **1280** and the height to **720**

❏ from the lower-left of the Recording Settings, click the **Gear**

❏ on the **Options** tab, review the default **Hotkey** (keyboard shortcut) needed to **Stop Recording**

If you know that the default iSpring Stop Hotkey is conflicting with another process on your computer, you can change the Hotkey to something else. When I worked on this book, I knew that the [**F10**] Hotkey would be a problem for me because another program uses that key. I changed the Stop recording Hotkey to [**Ctr**] [**s**], which was easy for me to remember. In the image below, you're seeing the application defaults, not my modifications.

❏ click the **OK** button

© 2020, IconLogic, Inc. All Rights Reserved.

Screen Recording Confidence Check

1. From the bottom of the **Recording Settings** area, click the red record button to **Start a new recording**.

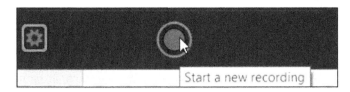

2. After the 3-2-1 countdown, work through the recording script exactly as you rehearsed it earlier. As a reminder, here are the steps you need to follow:

   ☐ in Notepad, click the **File** menu

   ☐ click the **Page Setup** menu item

   ☐ click the **Landscape** orientation button

   ☐ click the **OK** button

   ☐ click the **File** menu

   ☐ click the **Page Setup** menu item

   ☐ click the **Portrait** orientation button

   ☐ click the **OK** button

   ☐ click the recording process using the Hotkey you set up (the default is [**F10**])

   Once you finished the recording, the Screen Recording Complete screen appears. My favorite iSpring is also its most subtle: automatic Annotations.

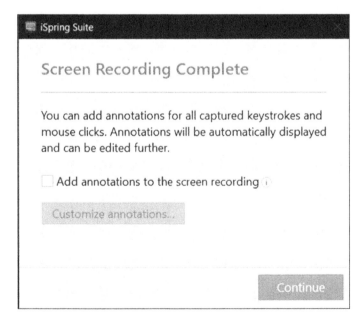

3. Select **Add annotations to the screen recording**.

4. Click the **Continue** button.

   The Recording you created opens. At this point, you can play it, edit it, or Save and return to the course.

5. Click the **Play** button.

How impressive is it that this tool adds the instructions (the Annotations) to the recording? This is the kind of feature I'm used to seeing in leading-edge eLearning development tools like Adobe Captivate and Articulate Storyline. Like those competing tools, the automatic Annotations can be easily edited via the Timeline at the bottom of the window.

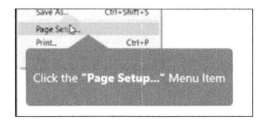

6. From the **Timeline** at the bottom of the screen, double-click any of the annotations and, from the **Format** tab on the Ribbon, change the appearance as you see fit.

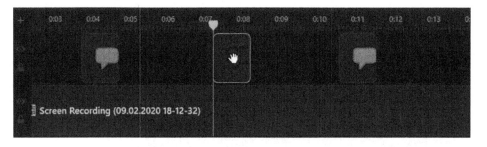

7. When finished, from the **Home** tab on the Ribbon, click **Save and return to course**.

8. Save and close the presentation.

© 2020, IconLogic, Inc. All Rights Reserved.

iCONLOGiC

"Skills and Drills" Learning

Module 5: Quizzing

In This Module You Will Learn About:

And You Will Learn To:

Creating Quizzes

Learning can be exhausting. If you think about it, there's only so much learning that can effectively occur over a set amount of time. As a professional trainer, I can force-feed information to my students. However, without regularly scheduled breaks, the ability of my students to both learn and retain information is minimized. Beyond breaks, I also encourage my learners to openly discuss with their classmates (and with me) what they learned during class. I've found that discussing the concepts taught in class greatly improves the students' experience, enhances understanding of the concepts, and increases retention of the material.

When it comes to eLearning, there isn't a live trainer and there aren't any classmates. How is a learner supposed to share the knowledge gained during an eLearning course when the learner is isolated? One answer is to add a quiz. In addition to measuring the effectiveness of course content, students are able to think about and recall what they learned as they answer questions presented in the quiz.

The iSpring QuizMaker includes a wonderful array of Question Types including Multiple Choice, True/False, Matching, Fill in the blank, Hotspot, and even Drag Drop. During the activities that follow, you'll get a chance to add a quiz and a few questions.

Guided Activity 25: Add a Quiz

1. Using PowerPoint, open the **QuizMe** file from the **iSpring9Data** folder.

2. Add a Quiz.

   ❏ select slide **10**

   ❏ from the **iSpring Suite** tab on the Ribbon, **Insert** group, click **Quiz**

iSpring QuizMaker opens.

   ❏ from the **Create** area, click **Graded Quiz**

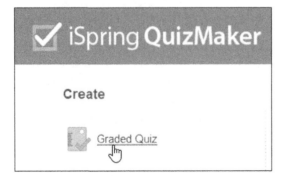

© 2020, IconLogic, Inc. All Rights Reserved.

3. Name the Quiz.

☐ from the **Home** tab on the Ribbon, **Quiz** group, click **Properties**

The Quiz Properties screen opens.

☐ from the list at the left, select **Main Properties**

☐ from the **Title and Size** area, change the **Quiz Title** to **PPE Quiz**

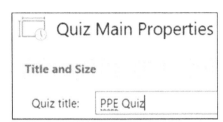

4. Set the quiz scoring properties.

☐ from the list at the left, select **Quiz Scoring**

☐ change the **Passing score** percentage to **50**

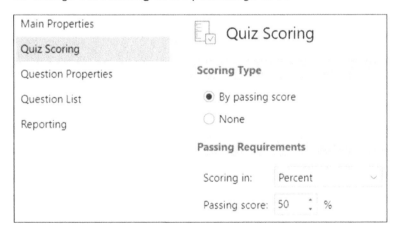

5. Set the point value per question.

☐ from the list at the left, select **Question Properties**

☐ change the **Points for a correct answer** to **50**

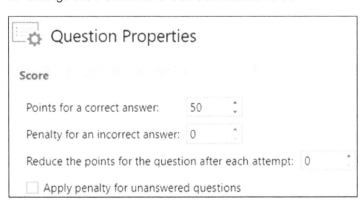

© 2020, IconLogic, Inc. All Rights Reserved.

6. Review the default Feedback Messages.

☐ ensure you're still viewing the Question Properties

☐ scroll down to the **Feedback** area

After a learner answers a question and submits the answer, feedback appears on the slide. The feedback that they will see comes from this area. Although you could easily edit this text, the default wording is fine, so you'll leave things as they are.

Feedback	
☑ Show feedback for graded questions	
☐ Show feedback for survey questions	
Correct:	That's right! You chose the correct response.
Incorrect:	You did not choose the correct response.
Partially Correct:	That's not exactly the correct response.
Try Again:	You did not choose the correct response. Please try again. You have %ANSWER_ATTEMPTS%
Answered:	Thank you for your answer!

☐ click the **Save** button

You are now back at the main QuizMaker screen, ready to add the quiz questions.

 © 2020, IconLogic, Inc. All Rights Reserved.

Guided Activity 26: Insert a Graded Question

1. Ensure that the **QuizMe** presentation is still open and that **QuizMaker** is running.

2. Add a Multiple Choice Question to the PPE Quiz.

   ❑ from the **Home** tab on the QuizMaker Ribbon, **Insert** group, click **Question** drop-down menu and choose **Multiple Choice**

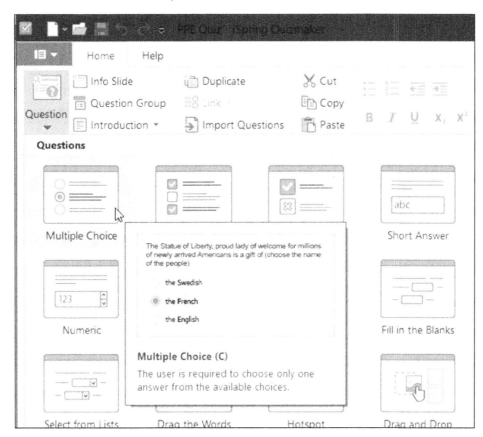

The **Multiple Choice Question** opens in Form View. This view provides all of the options needed to set up the question including the question, answers, feedback, and scoring. The other view, Slide View, provides a preview of what the quiz question will look like to learners.

3. Add the Question.

   ❑ replace the existing question text with **What is a PPE?**

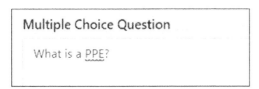

4. Add the Choices.

   ❑ replace the **Option 1** placeholder text with **Personal Protective Equipment**

   ❑ replace the **Option 2** placeholder text with **Prepared Protective Environment**

© 2020, IconLogic, Inc. All Rights Reserved.

□ replace the **Option 3** placeholder text with **Preferred Protective Equipment**

□ click where it says *Type to add a new choice* and type **Profound Prepared Effective**

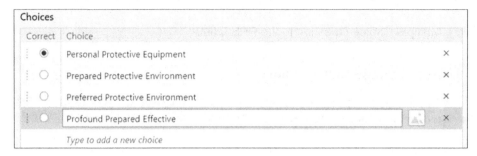

5. Select the correct answer.

□ click each of the radio buttons to the left of each choice

As you click, the radio button fills in indicating the choice is the correct answer.

□ click to the left of **Personal Protective Equipment** to set this choice as the correct answer

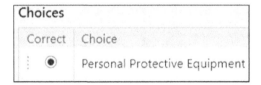

□ from the **Home** tab on the QuizMaker Ribbon, **Publish** group, click **Preview**

A preview of the quiz question opens. You'll learn how to improve the background image and overall layout next.

6. Close the preview.

© 2020, IconLogic, Inc. All Rights Reserved.

Guided Activity 27: Format a Question Slide

1. Ensure that the **QuizMe** presentation is still open and that **QuizMaker** is running.

2. Ensure that the What is a PPE multiple choice question is still open.

3. Use the presentation slide as the quiz background.

   ❑ from the left side of QuizMaker, click **Slide View**

   ❑ from the **Home** tab on the QuizMaker Ribbon, **Quiz** group, click **Player**

   The Player Controls open.

   ❑ from the top of the Player Controls, click **Features**

   ❑ from the Quiz Background area, select **Use presentation slide as quiz background**

   In the preview area, notice that your question and choices aren't lined up very well (the question is too high on the page).

   ❑ from the top of the Player Controls, click **Apply & Close**

4. Reposition question slide objects.

   ❑ still working in Slide View, drag the question slide elements until the question is formatted similarly to the image below

   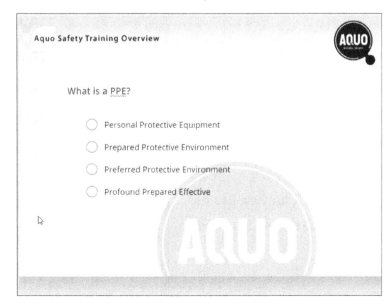

© 2020, IconLogic, Inc. All Rights Reserved.

Question Slide Confidence Check

1. Select **Form View**.

2. Insert another multiple choice question with the question and choices as shown below:

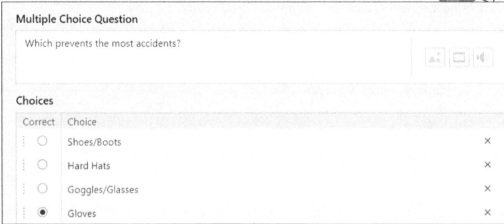

3. Format the slide similar to the image below.

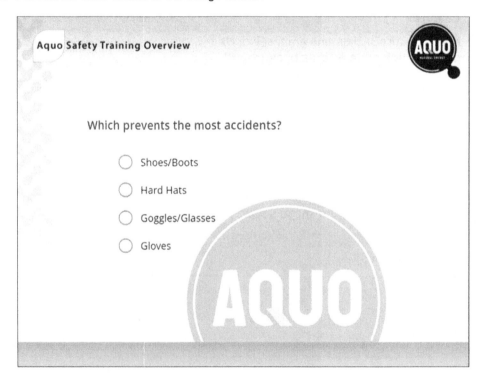

4. Preview and take the quiz.

5. After answering both questions, click View Results.

   You will learn how to format the Results slide next.

6. Close the Preview.

7. Save and return to the course.

 © 2020, IconLogic, Inc. All Rights Reserved.

Guided Activity 28: Customize the Quiz Results Slide

1. Ensure that the **QuizMe** presentation is still open.

2. Open the quiz.

    ☐ select slide **10**

    ☐ from the **iSpring Suite** tab on the Ribbon, **Insert** group, click **Quiz**

    The quiz you created earlier reopens for editing.

3. Edit the Quiz Results slide.

    ☐ from the Results area at the left, click **Quiz Results**

    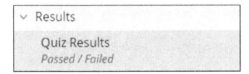

    ☐ from the Quiz Results area, click the **Failed** tab

    ☐ change the Failure message to **Sorry, you did not pass the quiz.**

    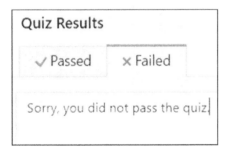

    ☐ switch to **Slide View**

    ☐ on the slide, select the **Review Quiz** button

    ☐ from the **Drawing Tools, Format** tab on the Ribbon, select any **Shape Style**

    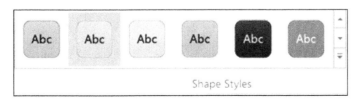

4. Save and return to the course.

Guided Activity 29: Hide a Slide

1. Ensure that the **QuizMe** presentation is still open.

2. Preview the entire presentation.

   The lesson plays correctly, and all is well. However, notice that all of the slides on the outline have names except the quiz. You'll fix that next.

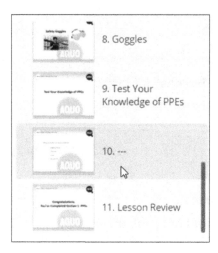

3. Close the Preview.

4. Name a slide.

   ❏ from the **iSpring Suite** tab on the Ribbon, **Presentation** group, click **Slide Properties**

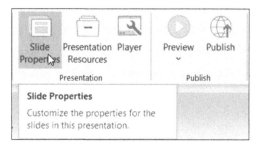

   The Slide Properties screen opens.

   ❏ click in the space to the right of slide **10** and type **Quiz Questions**

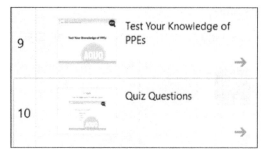

   ❏ from the top of the Slide Properties screen, click **Save and Close**

 © 2020, IconLogic, Inc. All Rights Reserved.

5. Preview the entire presentation.

   The Quiz Questions appear in the Outline with a proper name. However, as it now stands, learners could use the Outline to bypass the presentation and jump right to the quiz. From my perspective, if a learner wants to bypass the content and take the quiz right away, that's fine. If you'd like to hide the quiz behind other slides, you can make it accessible through a branch. You'll do that next.

6. Close the Preview.

7. Hide a slide.

   ❑ from the **iSpring Suite** tab on the Ribbon, **Presentation** group, click **Slide Properties**

   ❑ right-click slide 10 and choose **Hide**

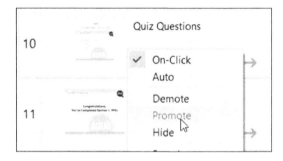

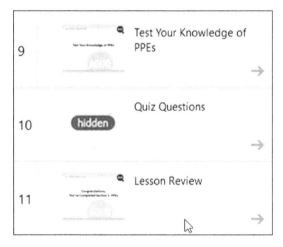

8. Save and close the Slide Properties.

9. Preview the entire presentation and notice that the quiz questions do not appear at all. At this point, there is no way to take the quiz.

10. Close the Preview.

NOTES

Guided Activity 30: Create a Branch

1. Ensure that the **QuizMe** presentation is still open.

2. Create a Branch.

   ☐ from the **iSpring Suite** tab on the Ribbon, **Presentation** group, click **Slide Properties**

   ☐ for slide **9**, click in word **Default** in the **Branching** column

   The Slide Branching Options open.

   ☐ from the **Forward branching** drop-down menu, choose **10. Quiz Questions**

   ☐ from the **Backward branching** drop-down menu, choose **8. Goggles**

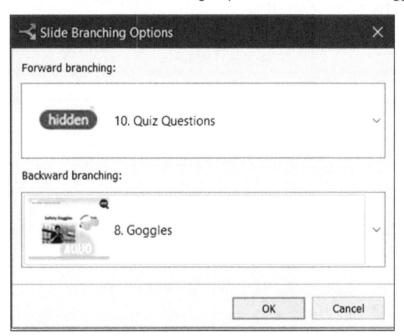

3. Demote slides.

   ☐ to the right of slide 4, click the **Demote** icon

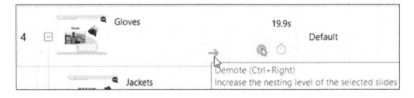

4. Demote slides **5**, **6**, **7**, and **8**.

5. Save and close the Slide Properties.

6. Preview the entire presentation and notice that the **demoted** slides still appear on the Outline but only after you get to the PPE slide. The **hidden** quiz questions never appear on the Outline but do start right after slide 9 thanks to the Branching you set up.

7. Close the Preview.

 © 2020, IconLogic, Inc. All Rights Reserved.

iCONLOGiC

"Skills and Drills" Learning

Module 6: Publishing

In This Module You Will Learn About:

- The Player, page 110
- Publish Locally, page 116
- Publish for an LMS, page 118

And You Will Learn To:

- Add a Presenter, page 111
- Customize the Player, page 112
- Publish as HTML5, page 116
- Publish a Project for Use in an LMS, page 119
- Create a Backup Copy of an iSpring Project, page 123

The Player

You've previewed your work several times during activities throughout this book. When the preview opens in your web browser, all of the content you created is contained within a shell—the Player. In addition to the PowerPoint slide, which takes up the majority of the Player, there's also a Sidebar area and a Bottom Bar (both are indicated in the image below). If the Sidebar sounds familiar, it should. You learned how to enable the Sidebar on page 62 so a video added via the **Manage Narration** dialog box would appear.

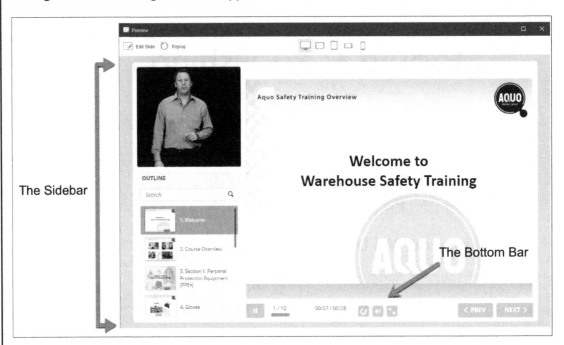

The Sidebar

The Bottom Bar

And there are additional Player options not shown in the image below such as a Contents area. You have significant control over the Player features that appear (only a few of the Player options have been made available up to this point), fonts that are used, overall layout, and colors. During the next few activities, you'll access the Player and customize it.

First, however, you'll add information about the Presenter. The information you add can appear on the Player.

© 2020, IconLogic, Inc. All Rights Reserved.

Guided Activity 31: Add a Presenter

1. Using PowerPoint, open the **PublishMe.pptx** file from the **iSpring9Data** folder.

2. Add a Presenter to the project.

   ☐ from the **iSpring Suite** tab, **Presentation** section, click **Presentation Resources**

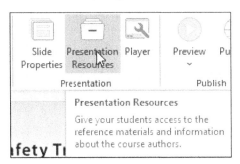

   The Presentation Resources dialog box opens.

   ☐ from the list of categories at the left, click **Presenters**
   ☐ from the bottom of the dialog box, click the **Add** button

   The **Edit Presenter Info** dialog box opens.

   ☐ in the **Name** field, type **Jim Stevens**
   ☐ in the **Job Title** field, type **Safety Manager**
   ☐ in the **Email** field, type **jim.stevens@aquo.com**

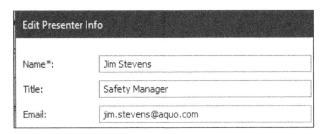

   ☐ click the **OK** button

   The new Presenter appears in the Presenters area.

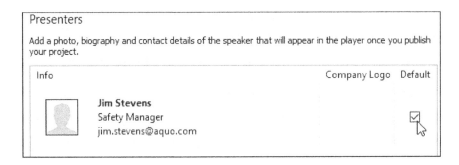

   ☐ from the right side of the dialog box, select **Default** (put a check in the box)
   ☐ click the **OK** button

Guided Activity 32: Customize the Player

1. Ensure that the **PublishMe** presentation is still open.

2. Preview the Entire Presentation.

   As the preview moves along, notice the appearance of the buttons in the Bottom Bar. Also notice that there's no mention of the Presenter that you just set up a moment ago. You'll change the colors next and enable the Presenter.

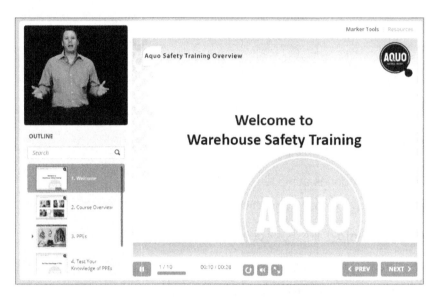

3. Close the preview.

4. Add the Presenter information to the Player.

   ☐ from the **iSpring Suite** tab on the Ribbon, **Presentation** section, click **Player**

   The Customize Player dialog box opens.

   ☐ from the top of the dialog box, click **Layout**

   The Layout properties appear along the left of the dialog box.

   ☐ from the lower left of the dialog box, **Presenter Info** drop-down menu, choose **On the Top Bar (Popup)**

© 2020, IconLogic, Inc. All Rights Reserved.

5. Modify the Top bar.

☐ from the top of the Customize Player dialog box, click **Top Bar**

The Top Bar properties appear at the left of the dialog box.

☐ from the list of **Buttons**, ensure **Marker Tools**

☐ from the list of **Buttons**, ensure **Presenter Info** is selected

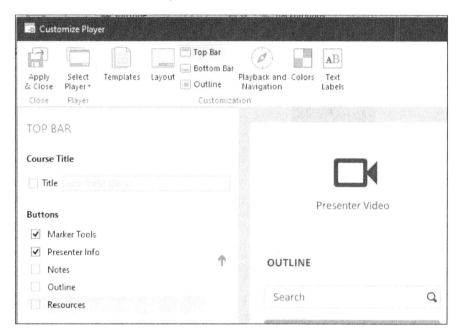

☐ from the list of **Buttons**, deselect **Resources**

6. Change the colors used in the Bottom Bar.

☐ from the top of the Customize Player dialog box, click **Colors**

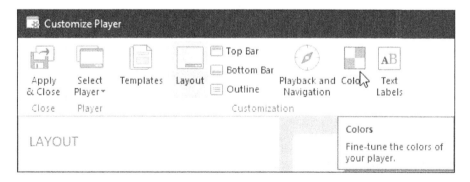

Color options appear down the left side of the dialog box.

☐ from the **Button/Inactive Tab** area, click the **Color Picker**

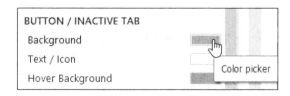

NOTES

© 2020, IconLogic, Inc. All Rights Reserved.

NOTES

☐ from just above the Cancel button, select the eyedropper tool

☐ position the eyedropper tool above the green color in the slide background and click

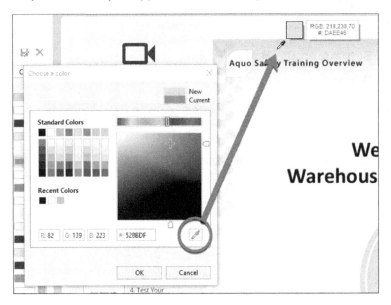

☐ click the **OK** button

The eyedropper "sucks up" the green color and instantly applies it to the buttons on the Bottom Bar. *How awesomely cool is that?*

7. From the top left of the dialog box, click **Apply & Close**.

© 2020, IconLogic, Inc. All Rights Reserved.

Player Confidence Check

1. Preview the Entire Presentation.

    As the preview moves along, notice the edited color of the buttons in the Bottom Bar.

2. From the top of the Player, explore the **Presenter Info** and **Marker Tools**.

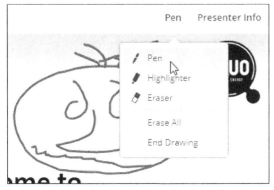

3. Close the preview.

4. Spend a few minutes exploring some of the other customization features you'll find in the Player. (Make any changes you like... it's your project.)

5. Save the project.

Publish Locally

I get asked this great question a lot: "What do my learners need to access content I've created with iSpring Suite." Beyond access to your content, all learners need to view your finished content is for you to publish, and to store the published assets in an accessible location (a Web server, a video streaming server, or a Learning Management System). Learners do NOT need to own PowerPoint or iSpring Suite. Instead, if they have access to your content, they need a free web browser and device that can view HTML5 and videos. Most modern desktop computers, laptops, tablets, and smart phones come with browsers and are fully capable for viewing HTML5 and videos. All you need to do is Publish your project and upload it to an appropriate location.

Guided Activity 33: Publish as HTML5

1. Ensure that the **PublishMe** presentation is still open.

2. Publish as HTML5.

    ❒ from the **iSpring Suite** tab on the Ribbon, **Publish** section, click **Publish**

    The Publish dialog box opens.

    ❒ from the list at the left, choose **My Computer**

    This option simply means that when the Publish process completes, the published assets will remain on your computer versus being uploaded to a remote location. Once published, you would be expected to either upload the published assets to their final destination or give them to a person or the department responsible for uploading the content.

    ❒ from the **Folder** area, click the **Browse** button

    ❒ navigate to the **iSpring9Data** folder

    ❒ open the **PublishProjectsHere** folder

    ❒ click the **Select Folder** button

Publish to My Computer		
Project name:	AquoSafetyDemo	
Folder:	∋s\iSpring9Data\PublishProjectsHere	Browse...
Output Options		
Format:	HTML5 Video	

© 2020, IconLogic, Inc. All Rights Reserved.

❏ from the Output Options, Format area, select **HTML5**

❏ from the lower right of the dialog box, click the **Publish** button

The project files are generated into output files that can be viewed on just about any kind of computer or mobile device.

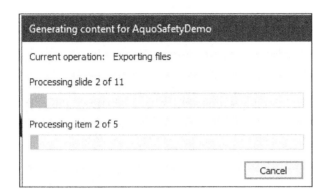

When the publishing process completes, you'll see the alert dialog box below.

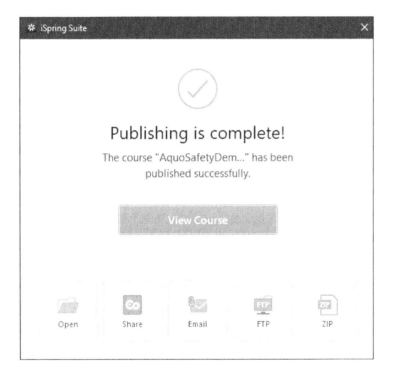

❏ click the **View Course** button

The published project opens in your default web browser.

Congratulations! You are now a published eLearning author!

3. Close the web browser and return to the PowerPoint presentation.

4. Close the Publishing Complete alert box.

Publish for an LMS

Later in this section you will publish a presentation so it can be uploaded into a Learning Management System (LMS). *But not so fast.* Before a lesson can be used with an LMS, you have to set up some reporting options and become familiar with the following terms and acronyms: SCORM, AICC, Experience API, cmi5, SCOs, and the Manifest File.

SCORM

Developed by public- and private-sector organizations, Sharable Content Object Reference Model (SCORM) is a series of eLearning standards that specify ways to catalog, launch, and track course objects. Courses and management systems that follow the SCORM specifications allow for sharing of courses among federal agencies, colleges, and universities. Although SCORM is not the only eLearning standard (AICC is another and it is addressed next), SCORM is one of the most common. There are two versions of SCORM: version 1.2, released in 1999, and version 2004.

AICC

Aviation Industry Computer-Based Training Committee (AICC) is an international association that develops guidelines for the aviation industry in the development, delivery, and evaluation of training technologies. When you publish your iSpring Suite lessons, you can specify SCORM or AICC compliance, but not both. Not sure which one to pick? Talk to your LMS provider for information on which one to use. When in doubt, consider that AICC is older and more established than SCORM, but SCORM is the standard most often used today.

Experience API

Today's learners are consuming eLearning content using a vast array of devices (PCs, Macs, and mobile devices, such as the Apple iPad). And learners are working outside of traditional LMSs. In spite of these challenges, educators still need to capture reliable data about the learner experience.

The problem with data collection is that you need a place to store and access it. And your learners need live access to the storage area so that they can send the data. As mentioned above, the most widely used LMS standard for capturing data is SCORM. SCORM allows educators to track such things as learner completion of a course, pass/fail rates, and the amount of time a learner took to complete a lesson or course. But what if a trainer needs to get scores from learners who are collaborating with other students using social media? What if the learners don't have access to the Internet?

The Experience API allows training professionals to gather detailed data about the learner experience as the learner moves through an eLearning course (either online or offline). According to the Experience API website, "the Experience API (also known as xAPI or TinCan) captures data in a consistent format about a person or group's activities from many technologies. Very different systems are able to securely communicate by capturing and sharing this stream of activities using xAPI's simple vocabulary."

cmi5

cmi5 uses the Experience API as a communications protocol. According to iSpring, it's the next generation of SCORM providing all the capabilities of SCORM and xAPI at the same time. Unlike with SCORM, cmi5 courses can be taken both online *or* offline meaning that students can take an eLearning course even when there's no Internet connection. (The learner's progress will be saved and sent to the LMS once an Internet connection is restored.)

© 2020, IconLogic, Inc. All Rights Reserved.

SCOs

Sharable Content Objects (SCOs) are standardized, reusable learning objects. An LMS can launch and communicate with SCOs and can interpret instructions that tell the LMS which SCO to show a user and when to show it. Why should you know what an SCO is? Actually, your iSpring Suite projects are SCOs once you enable reporting (which you will learn to do next).

Manifest Files

The Manifest file allows your published presentation to be used and launched from a SCORM 1.2- or 2004-compliant LMS. When you publish a presentation, you can have iSpring Suite create the Manifest file for you. The Manifest file that iSpring Suite creates contains XML tags that describe the organization and structure of the published project to the LMS.

Guided Activity 34: Publish a Project for Use in an LMS

1. Ensure that the **PublishMe** presentation is still open.

2. Enable LMS SCORM 1.2 Reporting options.

    ☐ from the **iSpring Suite** tab on the Ribbon, **Publish** section, click **Publish**

    ☐ from the list at the left, **LMS**

    ☐ from the **Learning Course Options** area, **LMS Profile** drop-down menu, choose **SCORM 1.2**

3. Set up the Manifest File.

    ☐ from the **Learning Course Options** area, click the **Customize** button

    The Manifest dialog box opens.

    ☐ from the **Type** drop-down menu, ensure **1.2** is selected

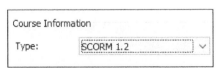

    SCORM 1.2, while an older standard, is still used by many LMSs today. When I publish content, I always try 1.2 first and use the other Types as needed.

❑ change the **Course Name** to **Aquo Safety**

In a typical LMS, there are **Catalogs** (a collection of courses), Courses (a collection of lessons), and **Lessons** (each individual iSpring project is a lesson once published). If you use the same Course Name when publishing each of your iSpring Suite projects, most LMSs will see the identical names and automatically group all of the lessons into the same Course.

❑ change the **Lesson title** field to **Personal Protective Equipment**

The Lesson title is seen by learners as they access the lesson on the LMS.

A Description is not required. Depending on the LMS you use, the text may or may not appear in the LMS. If the feature is not supported by the LMS, it will simply be ignored, You'll leave the Description blank for this lesson.

The Identifier can be a combination of letters and/or numbers. It is used by the LMS for cataloging purposes. Some developers never use the same Identifier twice and keep a log book of the Identifiers used by lesson.

❑ in the **Identifier** field, type **ppe_lesson_001**

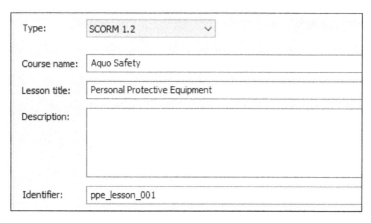

4. Set up the Progress and Completion criteria.

❑ from the bottom of the dialog box, click **Customize**

The Progress and Completion dialog box opens.

❑ from the **Report completion** area, **Report status to LMS as** drop-down menu, choose **Complete/Failed**

When the learner accesses the lesson through the LMS and takes the quiz, the score will be reported to the LMS; after the learner takes the quiz, the LMS displays Passed or Failed to the learner.

© 2020, IconLogic, Inc. All Rights Reserved.

5. From the **Graded items** area, notice that the quiz you set up earlier is being used for the scoring criteria.

6. From the **Total score** area, notice that the Max score is already set to **100**.

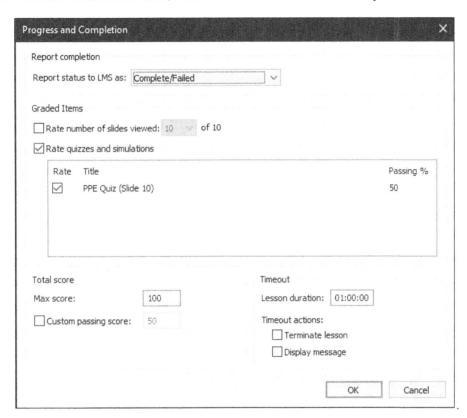

7. Click the OK button.

8. Click the Save button.

Publishing Confidence Check

1. Click the Publish button to finish the publishing process.

2. When the publishing process is complete, click the Open icon **Publishing is complete** screen.

3. The SCORM-compliant package you published is shown in the publish destination folder.

4. Return to iSpring Suite and dismiss the **Publishing is complete** screen.

5. Save and **close** the project.

6. Open the **iSpring Suite 9** Quick Start screen (click the Start button in Windows and type **iSpring**).

7. On the Quick Start screen, click **Books**.

8. From the Create From area, select **MS PowerPoint**.

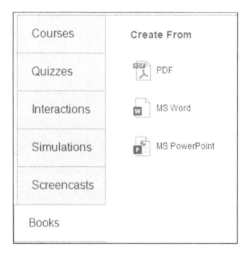

9. From the iSpring9Data folder, open **PublishMe.**

10. From the top of the screen, click the **Publish** button.

11. Publish the project using the default settings to **iSpring9Data** > **PublishProjectsHere**.

12. When the publish process is complete, **View** the Book. Although the videos won't play, there's no audio, and the interactions won't work, consider how awesome this output might work for other PowerPoint content you've got laying around. Pretty cool, eh?

13. Close the book, dismiss the Publish Complete screen, and close the Book tool.

© 2020, IconLogic, Inc. All Rights Reserved.

Share a Project

During this module (and late in module 1), you have learned how to publish your iSpring project. Publishing generates output files that learners need to view your content (via their own computer or mobile device and a free web browser).

If you want to edit the iSpring project, you need PowerPoint and the version of iSpring Suite used to create the project (or newer). If a colleague needs to edit the project on your behalf, he or she also needs PowerPoint and the version of iSpring Suite used to create the project (or newer). Your team member(s) will also need the iSpring project. Keep in mind that an project can be made up of several components including the PowerPoint presentation, interactions, videos, and audio files. To ensure that a team member has all of the required project assets needed to open and then edit the project, you could manually copy and paste everything and store them in a central location. However, I frequently hear from people that they've forgotten this asset or that and the iSpring project does not open correctly.

For peace of mind, I recommend using iSpring Suite's **Share** feature. When you share a project, iSpring copies all of the project's assets to one location for you and then zips them together into one tidy package.

Guided Activity 35: Create a Backup Copy of an iSpring Project

1. Using PowerPoint, reopen the **PublishMe** presentation.

2. Create a project backup for sharing with team members.

    ☐ choose **File > Share**

    ☐ choose **Share iSpring Suite Project**

    ☐ click the **Export Project**

    The Export iSpring Suite Project dialog box opens.

    ☐ click the **Browse** button and open the **iSpring9Data** folder

    ☐ click the **Select Folder** button

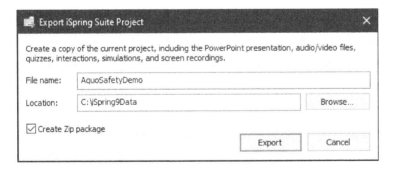

    ☐ ensure that **Create Zip Package** is selected

    ☐ click the **Export** button

NOTES

NOTES

All of the project files are zipped into one file. At this point, you can email the file to a colleague or copy it to a shared resource/server like Dropbox or SharePoint. The team member could then unzip, view, and edit the project (as long as they had access to PowerPoint and iSpring Suite).

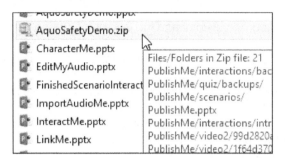

3. Return to PowerPoint.

4. Save and close the presentation.

      © 2020, IconLogic, Inc. All Rights Reserved.

Index

© 2020, IconLogic. All Rights Reserved.

Made in the USA
Coppell, TX
08 March 2020

16631062R10079